Baking

Recipes

for Kids

Eva

Table of Contents

CHAPTER ONE

LET'S WALK INTO THE WORLD OF BAKING!

Baking is a world of its own and many people have decided to walk in this world by showing off the skills nature freely gives to them. The world of baking has welcomed scholars, professionals, and craft men and women and they have help to expand the world of baking and this has let people to wonder if baking is an art or science.

Even today's children in the world of baking ask the question. To some it is the art of designing new shapes and being creative with the cake just to get an end result. Also it is a culinary art of using kitchen utensils to make artistic images, designs, and so on. While as a science on the other hand, it involves being correct in our measurement. We have to use precise ratios of particular ingredients in particular proportions. It is important to know that wrong measurements will not give us a successful baked good. So in order to get these proportions right, we need to measure them correctly.

This book exposes us to the baking world for little children. It reveals how children can walk into the world of baking with little or no experience. The first aspect exposes us to the basics of learning how to bake and the tools to be used. Some of the basics are; the secrets behind baking, the best way to melt butter for baking, soften butter quickly and easily, how to crack and separate the perfect egg, test for doneness with a toothpick, how to make an aluminum foil sling, and so on. These and many more that are used by bakers, chefs and the likes will be discussed in details below.

The book also exposes all children to the practical aspects of baking. We will do this by explaining the time taken to mix, bake and even the number of people each round of baking can feed. We will also explain different types of recipes and how to go about them. I know you love cookies kids. Some of the cookies recipes are; fudgy mint cookies, batter cookies, peanut butter cookies, rocky road cookie cups, pixie dust cookies, giant sharing cookies, peanut butter kiss cookies, earth cookies and many more. But we will learn how to bake cakes and bars too and a lot more. Just make sure to have some fun while you are at it.

THE SECRETS OF SUCCESSFUL BAKING

Baking has got some secrets. As a beginner or a professional in the world of baking you should know these secrets. We will talk about three of them here. These secrets include checking out your ingredients, using oil in cake recipes and the secret to successful scones.

Checking Out Your Ingredients

Once you start baking, you have to stick to it until you finish. It is just like going to school. Once you are in class, you have to stay until the end. Immediately you go into your kitchen, you have to remain there until you are done with the baking, be it chips, cookies or cakes. This means that you will be using whatever you have with you in the kitchen. It is important to note that you need to get the necessary ingredients ready for use. In the same way you cannot enter the classroom without a pen, you cannot go into the kitchen or baking room with incomplete ingredients. Your recipes will guide you on what you need for each baking session. So I implore you to gather the necessary ingredients before baking so that you won't get it wrong.

Using The Right Baking Recipes

After putting a lot of efforts into baking, one expect to have the best output. This may not be the case if you use the wrong baking recipes. You cannot bake a cake and expect to see a pizza. The recipes in this book will explain to you how to bake different types of goodies. All you have to do is choose which one you would like to eat, and find the right recipe.

The recipes are different even where they look similar. For example, the quantity that you need might be different from one to another. You may need a specific type of oil or butter. So be careful as you follow the recipes.

The Secret To Successful Scones

When cutting out your scones from the dough, you should be careful to follow the instructions in the recipe. When doing this, make sure your hand is straight when cutting. Don't twist your hand because if you do, you will miss the perfect shape you are trying to calve and it won't make successful dough. It is important to know that before cutting the dough, you have to dip the cutter in flour to prevent it from sticking, and at the end you will have a masterpiece.

THE BAKING

Like other speaking languages, baking speaks too and that is what this book is trying to reveal to us. We will achieve a great deal more if we understand the language of baking. Some important terms are; measure, flour, preheat, knead, dough while some minor ones are; mix, stir, whisk, add, etc. If you're learning a language, you have to follow the instruction. It's the same with baking. You must follow the recipe which is a list of instructions for baking our goodies. If you understand the baking language, you won't miss out in the process. Below are some of the languages in baking.

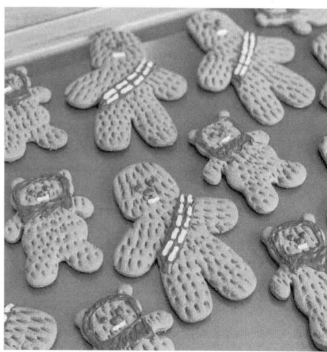

Measure This is basically the first thing to know in baking because if you do not measure correctly, the whole process will be useless. It is very important to measure your ingredients before baking. Measuring is using the right amount of ingredients. The unit of measurement in different countries differs, so I implore you to check for the right one your country is using. It is also important to know the conversion of standard unit.

Flour We may be able to do away with some ingredients while baking, but not flour. Flour is one of the most important baking ingredients. You will soon find that flour is a part of all the baking recipes we will be talking about in this book. Flour is a light, fluffy, white powder that is used to make cookies, chips, bread, cakes and so on. The commonly used flour is made from wheat.

Preheat To preheat means to allow your oven get warm before the normal baking starts. You will find that many of the recipes tell you to preheat the oven before you start baking. You will need to set the oven to the heating temperature that is written in your recipe

Knead To knead simply means to create circle-like dough with the available dough mixture. One can easily knead bread from the dough on a flat surface. To be sure that the dough does not stick, add little flour on the dough that you placed on a flat surface. Now you can knead with ease and create beautiful circle-like images.

Dough

I know you have been asking what is a dough? Dough is the combination of two different mixtures of wet (e.g buyer, sugar, egg etc) and dry (flour, salt, etc) ingredients that is used in baking. Dough may be made of flour, water, oil, sugar, baking powder, baking soda, and eggs. Dough is the end product of the mixture of these ingredients and the richness of the dough depend largely on the recipes used.

ENCYCLOPEDIA OF INGREDIENT

An encyclopedia of ingredients is talking about the totality of the ingredients used in cooking and not just the baking world. We shall concern ourselves to the baking world. Encyclopedia of ingredient helps us to understand the basic foundation of an ingredient and how it is to be used or apply. It explains and differentiates similar type of ingredients and when to use them. It also arranges essential ingredients and non-essential ingredients, and regards some as spices.

Similar ingredients

Some ingredients look the same. We are lucky! The encyclopedia helps us to differentiate them. Some may taste almost the same to the tongue but there is difference when using them in the baking world. They include table salt and salt, sugar and granulated sugar, vegetable oil and virgin oil, baking soda and baking powder, flour and wheat flour, and so on. It is easy to mistake one of the ingredients for another. The encyclopedia tells us when and how to use each one.

Essential ingredients

The encyclopedia explains that some ingredients are essential and we cannot do without them. Good examples are flour, salt, and so on.

Spices

Some of these ingredients though little in nature are regarded as the icing ingredients. They are used at the end of any baking. Their physical nature makes some people to downplay them by not using them but the encyclopedia says that they are useful in our cooking.

WEIGH & MEASURE SECRETS

Measurement is one of the first things to know in baking. Wrong measurement of ingredients makes a cake turn out too thick or smaller than expected. It may also crack. Let's learn some secrets that would help us know how to measure correctly.

Knowing the Weight of a cup of flour

There are different ways to measure our ingredients though some of them won't give us accurate measurements like the scooping and spooning and level off. The one that seems accurate and that I would tell you to try is weighing with digital or non-digital scale.

The main thing you need to know is that a cup of all-purpose flour weighs 125 to 130 grams. The exact weight will differ across different brands of flour, but if you use 130 grams you'll be alright. You must try to be accurate when measuring during baking.

Here are some weighing/measuring

Scooping or spooning

This type of measurement is cheap and common but it may be unreliable. All you need to do is use a small cup to scoop or spoon the ingredients before pouring them into a mixing bowl. The problem with this method is that the cup cannot be accurately measured.

Level off

This will not be explained further it is just for the record keeping. This method depend on a knife to scrape along the surface edge of the cup horizontally, thereby limiting the ingredients to go above the edge of the cup and making it a flat surface.

Weighing with digital or non-digital scale

This method uses a weighing scale to measure the required ingredients to be used for baking. The scaling measurement can either be a digital or non-digital scale. This is the most accurate type of measurement. With this method, you don't have to guess the quantity of each ingredient.

FREQUENTLY ASKED QUESTIONS

Baking is full of wonders and this has made a lot of people to ask questions of how are these wonders performed. I have once asked these questions too, and I am sure your mommy has. I know that new comers to this world will want to ask the same questions. Let's quickly answer some of your important questions.

How can I get my egg broken properly?

Everyone misses out on how to crack an egg when they are baking for the first time. You may think that you know how to crack an egg but wait until it is time to start baking. All you need to do is to look for a flat surface area to gently hit the egg open and separate the egg yolk from the egg white. Don't allow the shell to drop inside the bowl.

What if I use butter that is not of room temperature?

Using butter that is not of room temperature will not make your ingredients to stick. The butter will be too hard and this will affect your baking because it will not take shape. So it is advisable to use the required ingredient that is in the recipe.

Must I go to catering school before I will know how to bake?

You do not need to go to any catering school before you can be able to bake. All that is important is that you follow the required recipes given. The recipes are your instructions for doing it right. So obey all the steps like you would obey mommy. I am not saying going to catering school is bad. Besides going there will make you more professional and it can make you have a catering service

Can I use regular salted butter instead of unsalted butter?

Follow your recipe strictly if you want to get the required results. Using salted butter will add a lot of salt to your baking but using the unsalted butter that was recommended will help you to regulate the amount of salt in your final goodies. So I will always recommend that you use unsalted butter.

Top 5 "Must Do's" Before Baking (Prep Step)

I will show you five steps you need to complete before you begin baking. If you want your goodies to come out nicely, you have to follow the preparation steps properly. My friend once called me to help her buy flour on my way home because she did not know that her flour would not be enough before she starting her baking. This is an example of what could happen if you do not prepare properly before you begin your baking. I want you to avoid this kind of results by following the preparatory steps to baking.

Read the recipe

The first thing to do is to go through the list of recipes you will need for baking. Make sure the ingredients available are the same as the ones prescribed in the recipe. This is important because it will help to get the perfect output.

Your ingredients must be at room temperature (26°C-28°C)

It is important to know that all ingredients must be at room temperature in other to get the required results. Though sometimes room temperature may change due to the weather, we should know that for our baking to start properly, our ingredients should be between 26°C to 28°C.

Measure out your ingredients

Take time to measure your ingredients and make sure you are using the best method of measurement which is digital or non-digital scale. This will help us measure our flour correctly.

Preheat the oven

In every recipe an instruction is given on the degree the oven needs to be heated before baking commences. You should follow what is stated in your recipe. Tell mommy to help you with the oven settings.

Choose and prepare the right pan

Always choose the right pan when you bake because baking increases in volume while in the oven. If you use a smaller pan, your baking can overflow. After you have gotten the right pan, grease it with butter and dust it with flour. Make sure you tap the pan while rotating it to get rid of the excess flour.

Once you have done all these steps, you can start preparing your recipe.

THE BEST WAY TO MELT BUTTER FOR BAKING

There are series of ways we can melt our butter or bring it to room temperature before we use it. One great way to melt butter is to cut the butter into smaller pieces and put it in a fry pan. You then allow heat from the fire to steam it. You can also cut it into smaller pieces and put it in the microwave which is a bit faster.

These two methods are okay but I use a different method because if you use any of these, you will have to heat the butter and that will temper with the strength and nutrition of the butter. The best way to melt butter is the one explained below;

Allow it to dissolve some hours before baking time

The nutrients and the strength of the butter will remain the same if you use this method. Remember that you need these nutrients to grow. So here is what you do to make your butter soft. Spread it out on a flat surface and place it close to the oven or place it on the counter for about 2-3 hours. Cut the butter into smaller pieces. The weather will melt it if it is hot enough. The heat from the oven can also melt the butter.

SOFTEN BUTTER QUICKLY AND EASILY

If you want to make the butter soft without melting it, these other methods are a great way to do that. Although there are a lot of different ways to achieve this, we will be talking about three of them.

Use the frying pan

The first thing to do is to cut the butter into smaller chunks and set it in a frying pan. Turn on the heat of the fire. Use a spoon to stir the butter in the pan. Check and turn the other side of the butter to expose it to heat and make sure the heat from the fire is between 28-36°c.

Use the frying pan

The first thing to do is to cut the butter into smaller chunks and set it in a frying pan. Turn on the heat of the fire. Use a spoon to stir the butter in the pan. Check and turn the other side of the butter to expose it to heat and make sure the heat from the fire is between 28-36°c.
Use the Microwave
 This does not take long as it is one of the fastest methods of melting butter. All you need to do is cut the butter into smaller pieces and place it inside a bowl. Put the bowl inside the microwave for some minutes and watch as it takes shape. Remember you can only get a faster result if the butter is cut into small cubes first.

Use hot water

This is another method of melting butter to room temperature. It requires both the microwave and hot water. All that is needed is to cut the butter into pieces and keep it aside. Put water in a container inside the microwave to steam. Take the steamed water out and place the butter inside it. Watch as the butter takes its shape.

HOW TO CRACK AND SEPARATE THE PERFECT EGG

Newbies to the world of baking find it difficult to crack an egg without having its shell inside their solution. I am sure you find that hard too. Each time you crack the egg, its shell enters into the egg white in your bowl. This is a no no for baking. So, you have to learn the right way to do it. Most people crack egg by the edge of the bowl and one problem with cracking eggs on the side of the bowl is that it forces the cracked shell into the egg whites and makes the egg yolk scatter.

Here's how to crack an egg properly!

lat surface

The best way to crack an egg is to do it on a flat surface. This will help you to properly separate the egg yolk from the whites.

The rim of a bowl

Here you have to crack the egg open with a gentle hit on the rim of a bowl. You then wait for the egg to open before you start pouring it out into the bowl.

Once the egg is cracked and it is wide open, all you need to do is to separate the egg yolk from the egg white. If you can use the shell to separate it fine, but if you cannot please try to use your hand to systematically push the yolk to your other hand while the white is on the hand with the shell.

TEST FOR DONENESS WITH A TOOTHPICK

To check for doneness in our cake requires a simple but special way of knowing if the cake is ready to eat. There are different types of tools used to check if our savory goods are ready but here we stick to the use of toothpick. When the required time for baking is almost over, gradually remove the cake, cookie, pizza or bars and insert a toothpick in its middle. It might come out with the following results;

Sticky: If it is sticky and moist, and you have some of the cake or cookie on your toothpick, then it is not done yet. Stick the pan back in the oven for a few more minutes, and repeat the test. This is looking more solid, but it's not done yet

.

Doneness: On the other hand, if your toothpick comes out clean and neat, then the cake is done and ready to eat.

You must know that it is not all your goodies that the toothpick test can work for. Some cakes can be moist in the middle when they are ready but your recipe will tell you what to do.

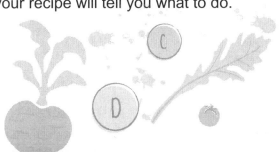

HOW TO MAKE AN ALUMINUM FOIL SLING

With an aluminum foil sling, we can keep from hurting our hands when we touch the hot pot. It will help us lift our pot out whenever we need to. The only item that is needed to make this sling is a heavy duty aluminum foil. Though there are other types of sling and any item can be used but we chose this because it lasts long.

Here's how to make one:

➤ Use your ruler to measure out 20-24 inches out of the bulk of aluminum foil you have available.
➤ Place it on a flat surface and fold it in half.
➤ Then, fold it on itself again.
➤ Press it down very flat. Try to carry it with the pot to see if it is ready for use.
➤

HOW TO MAKE AN ALUMINUM

With an aluminum foil sling, we can keep from hurting our hands when we touch the hot pot. It will help us lift our pot out whenever we need to. The only item that is needed to make this sling is a heavy duty aluminum foil. Though there are other types of sling and any item can be used but we chose this because it lasts long.

Here's how to make one:

- ▶ Use your ruler to measure out 20-24 inches out of the bulk of aluminum foil you have available.
- ▶ Place it on a flat surface and fold it in half.
- ▶ Then, fold it on itself again.
- ▶ Press it down very flat. Try to carry it with the pot to see if it is ready for use.

How To Use Your Foil Sling To Get Pans Out From Our Instant Pot

After you have made your sling, put it under your pot or pan. Lift the pot or pan and lower it gently into the instant pot using the sling. Unroll your aluminum foil sling again to gently lift out your finished food.

HOW TO GREASE A PAN FOR CAKE OR ANY RECIPE

Greasing with butter and flour

I have witnessed series of times how people poorly greased their pan before baking and I have always taught them the right thing to do. Remember! The goal of it all is for the pan not to stick to the cake or whatever you are baking.

There are several ways to grease your pans before baking. Some of them are using butter and flour, using butter and sugar, using nonstick cooking spray and using foil or parchment and many more but we will talk about three methods here.

Before you start baking, you need to make sure that your pan is properly greased with butter. It is a ritual that must be performed before baking begins. When you use butter, make sure it is applied all round the pan, at the bottom and sides, using the stick. You can also use a baking brush and it is very convenient to use. When you are through rubbing the butter splash around the pan, pour some flour into it. This will help to hold the baking item properly.

Greasing with butter and

Here you can use a paper towel to apply the butter if you feel it is more convenient for you. Do it thoroughly as you did with the butter and flour. After that, sprinkle your sugar on it. Try to let the sugar stick to the butter you just applied. Roll the pan over again and again to enable the sugar stick to the butter. You can choose to use your hand. This will allow you feel it if there is any missing spot to be greased.

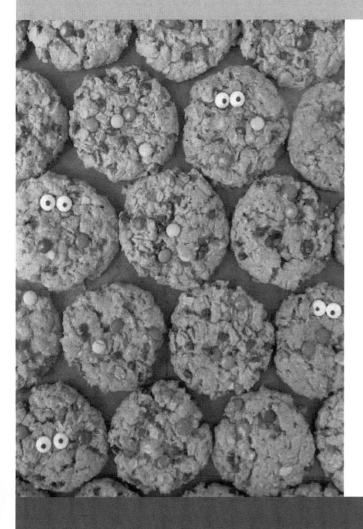

Using nonstick cooking spray

This is an advanced way of greasing our pan. This type of cooking spray comes in a beautiful cylinder and it is handy. One can easily hold and use it. All you have to do is to get a cooking spray and spray it inside the pan. Then your pan is ready for use.

HOW TO SHRED YOUR OWN CHEESE

People don't know how to shred their cheese even when they have a food shredder. Here I will try to explain how to use a shredder to shred your food or ingredients before baking. You can shred your ingredients the local way but this will make you have tired arms or get exhausted because you won't be as fast as the shredder. Most food processors will come with a handy attachment that will shred a block of cheese in seconds.

All you need to do is take a bowl and put the item that you want to shred inside it. Place the shredder on it. Exert some pressure on the shredder. You will see it perform magic. Or you can place the shredder inside the bowl and place the item on it. Apply pressure on it and try to swing it left and right. Do the swinging for a while.

Benefits Of Shredding Our Cheese

► It Saves Money When we shred cheese by ourselves, it gives us the sense of belonging and it also encourages us to save more thereby putting the money that is supposed to be used to shred cheese for something else.

Shredded Cheese Tastes Better

Cheese shredded by us looks more fresh and tastes better. This makes us to know that we can actually do it our way. This is important to baking.

► It reduces other additional ingredients that might be added when you shred it outside.
► Exposure to the sun and other pollution is also reduced.

TOOLS THAT MAKE YOUR WORK MORE EFFICIENT

In the world of baking, every tool is important but there are some that are indispensable because they are on every recipe, and they also add to the beauty of your job. Some of these tools are knives, bake ware, kitchen basic, small appliances, prep tools, baking tools, and so on.

You must know that some prep tools are very important and cannot be discarded so easily. You must have them in your kitchen before you begin baking.

How to shred

Knife

This is one the most important tools. It is used in cutting, fitting or designing cookies. It comes in different shapes and types. Some types are the all purpose knife, chef knife, straight cutting knife, paring knife, and so on. Our knife can do the slicing, dicing, chopping, and mincing of any ingredient in any recipe.

Bake ware

Bake ware are the materials used to do the actual baking activity and they play a major role in the life of a baker. They include the oven, pressure pot, wire rack, and so on. Without the bake ware, baking becomes useless. This is because the process of using bake ware adds beauty to the cake, cookies or whatever you are baking.

Kitchen basics

Kitchen basics are the tools used to add beauty to the baking process. Some of the basics are fork, kitchen scissors, toothpick, baking brush, and so on.

Preparatory tools

These tools are basically the foundation to proper and perfect baking. They help you with things like measurement and mixing of ingredients. You have to be sure you have them. One cannot do without using these tools. Some of them are, measuring scale, mixing bowl and cup, parchment paper, and so on.

CHAPTER TWO

MUFFIN, OTHER BREAKFAST TREATS SWEET FRENCH TOAST

Serving: 3 People
Baking Time: 20 minutes
Plus Cooling Time: 20 minutes

Ingredients

1/2 Tablespoon of Maple Syrup
1 Teaspoon of Vanilla Extract
1 Teaspoon of Ground Cinnamon
1/3 Cup Cornflakes Cereal
Crumbled 8 Slices Of White Bread
2 Tablespoons of Confectioner's
Sugar
3 Eggs
1/4 Cup Milk

Equipment

Griddle/Frying Pan
Bowl

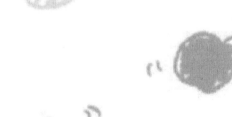

Direction

1. Break the eggs into a bowl and mix with the maple syrup, milk, cinnamon, and vanilla.
2. Stir for some time and crumble little cornflakes into the pan.
3. Keep stirring till it mixes well.
4. After that, add the bread slices in the mix and allow it to soak for about two to three minutes.
5. Next, heat a frying pan just a little over medium heat and place the slices of bread in it.
6. As you allow it to cook well and turn brown gradually, get the confectioner's sugar and sprinkle it all over.
7. Wait for it to get burned a bit further, and that's it.
8. Your Sweet French Toast is ready!

SAVORY FRENCH TOAST

Serving: 4 people
Baking Time: 4 minutes
Plus Cooling Time: 9 minutes

Ingredients

1/3 Cup Grated Parmesan Cheese
4 Eggs
¼ Cup Milk
1 Tablespoon Butter
Ground Black Pepper
4 Slices of Whole Wheat Bread.
Equipment
Frying Pan
Bowls

Directions

1. Get a bowl, a shallow one, if you can.
2. Break the eggs into it, pour in the milk, add the Parmesan cheese, and the black pepper then mix them properly until it becomes fluffy and light. This should take about one minute.
3. Heat a frying pan and melt butter into it.
4. Next, you should thrust both sides of each of the slices of bread into the mixture and place it   on the heating frying pan.
5. Take it out and place it on a plate.
6. You can now enjoy your toast!

PANEER BREAD ROLLS

Serving: 6 People
Baking Time: 10 minutes
Plus Cooling Time: 15 minutes

Ingredients

Small Onion (Beautifully Chopped)
1 Cup Crumbled Paneer
¼ Teaspoon Powdered Cumin/Jeera
½ Teaspoon Ginger Garlic Paste
1 Teaspoon Tomato Sauce/Ketchup
A Little Bunch Of Coriander (Well Chopped)
4 Slices Of Fresh White Bread
Butter
½ Teaspoon Red Chili Powder
Salt
½ Teaspoon Garam Masala.

Equipment
Frying Pan
Bowl

Directions

1. Get a clean, full bowl and put the crumbled paneer in it.
2. In the bowl, create a mix of the chili powder, well-chopped coriander, chopped onions, salt, cumin, and the garam masala in moderate quantities.
3. Use your fingertips to mix correctly, and then add the ketchup/tomato sauce and the ginger garlic paste as you continue mixing with your fingers.
4. Now get the bread and remove the crusts from it. Start rolling the bread.
5. After rolling the bread slice, add about one teaspoon of filling on one end. Ensure that you apply the filling properly so that it blends in well and then do the same with other slices.
6. Get a heated pan and toast the bread lightly till it turns brown. Serve it hot with some tomato sauce.

CHEESE CHILI TOAST

Serving: 4 People
Baking Time: 15 minutes
Plus Cooling Time: 20 minutes

Ingredients

finely-chopped Clove Garlic
Butter
Cheddar Mozzarella Cheese
well-chopped Capsicum
Teaspoon of Crushed Pepper
Salt
Finely-chopped Green Chili
White Bread Slices

Equipment

Pan
Bowl

Direction

start

1. Mix the whole of the mozzarella cheese, the capsicum, garlic, and the green chili.

2. Add the pepper and salt, then mix well so all the ingredients can create an elegant combination.

3. After mixing, put the bowl aside.

4. Apply the butter and toast on the bread slices till it becomes crispy.

5. Cut the bread in halves and spread butter on the other part and top it with mixed cheese.

6. Get the topped bread placed on a pan and cover it with a lid for it to cook on a mild flame till the melting of the cheese is complete. This will take about five to eight minutes.

7. Your cheese chili toast is ready to be served. You can include chili flakes and oregano toppings when serving.

CORN CAPSICUM SANDWICH

Serving: 3 People
Baking Time: 15 minutes
Plus Cooling Time: 30 minutes

Ingredients

Salt
Butter
10 - 12 Slices Of Bread
1 Cup Boiled Sweet Corn Kernels
85 Grams of Finely-chopped Bell Pepper (Capsicum)
1 Teaspoon of Crushed Black Pepper
Processed or Cheddar Cheese (25 Grams)

Equipment

Bowl
Pan

Directions

Pour all the ingredients except the bread and butter into a clean, wide bowl and mix them well.

Spread some butter and the corn capsicum stuffing on the bread slices.

Spread another slice of bread with butter and place it in a sandwich maker or oven.

Allow it to grill for some time till it becomes crispy.

Remove and slice them after waiting for some minutes.

Now your capsicum sandwich is ready.

Serve it with a coriander chutney or with tomato ketchup.

CHEESE CUTLET

Serving: 4 People
Baking Time: 25 minutes
Plus Cooling Time: 35 minutes

Ingredients

4 Boiled Potatoes
300 Grams of Paneer (Cottage Cheese)
6 Finely-chopped Green Chili
3 Slices of Bread
Salt
Bread Crumbs
2 Tablespoons of Well-chopped Coriander
1 Neatly-chopped Onion
¾ Cup Finely-chopped Cabbage
¾ Cup of Plain Flour
Oil
Tomato Ketchup

Equipment:

Bowl

Directions

1. Mash your potatoes until it blends well
2. Crumble the cheese and wait for 2 minutes
3. Soak the slices of bread in clean water and squeeze the water out
4. Get a clean bowl and pour in the mashed potatoes, the crumbled cheese, the slices of bread and onions, the well chopped chilies and cabbage
5. Add little salt.
6. Create your cutlets.
7. Dip the cutlets you have built into a combination of flour and add about 12 teacups of water
8. Roll the cutlets into bread crumbs and deep in hot oil for it to fry for some minutes.
9. You can now serve with the tomato ketchup topping.

CHEESE AND CELERY SANDWICHES

Serving: 4 People
Baking Time: 5 minutes
Plus Cooling Time: 5 minutes

Ingredients

8 Slices of Bread
4 Lettuce Leaves
1 Large Tomato (To Be Thinly Sliced)
Salt
Freshly Ground Pepper
2 Tablespoons of Mayonnaise
¼ Cup Cheese Spread
1 Clove of Garlic (Grated)
2 Finely-chopped Springs of Onions (With Greens)
1 Tablespoon of Finely-chopped Celery

Equipment:

Bowl

Directions

1. Mix the ingredients well in a bowl
2. Apply the mix on the slices of bread, alongside one large lettuce leaf on each slice.
3. Add some of the sliced tomatoes, and add sprinkles of the ground pepper and salt.
4. Then sandwich it with another slice of bread, and continue the same process for as many sandwiches you want to make.
5. Enjoy your sandwiches.

CARROT AND CHEESE FINGERS

Serving: 12 People
Baking Time: 10 minutes
Plus Cooling Time: 20 minutes

Ingredients

2 Teaspoons of Tomato Ketchup
Toasted Bread (4 Slices)
1 Cup of Grated Carrot
¾ Cup of Grated Processed Cheese
2 Tablespoons of Soft Butter
Salt

Equipment:

Bowl, Spatula

 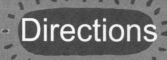 Directions

1. Put all of the carrot, cheese, butter, and the tomato ketchup together so that they form a mix
2. Add salt and taste.
3. If you get the desired feeling, you can keep the mix aside.
4. Now that your mix is ready, divide it into four equal portions.
5. Get your bread slices and spread a part of the mixture on each slice.
6. Get the cheese you have left and have it sprinkled over the bread slices.
7. Now it's time to bake.
8. Set your oven at 200°c for ten minutes.
9. After you have finished cooking, get each of the toast and cut it into three pieces (make them equal).
10. That's all about it, and when you're done, you can serve and eat even immediately.

VEGETABLE SANDWICH

Serving: 2 People
Baking Time: 10 minutes
Plus Cooling Time: 15 minutes

Ingredients

1 Tablespoon of Oil
4 Slices of Bread
1 Tablespoon of Finely-chopped Garlic
2 Tablespoons/Scoops of Butter
1 Pinch of Tumeric
Salt
½ Teaspoon of Cumin
1 Cup of Mixed Vegetables (including Carrot, Onions, Corn, Beans, and Capsicum)
2 Green Chilies
1 Large Tomato (Finely-chopped and Mashed)
2 Tablespoons of Coriander Leaves
½ - ¾ Tablespoons of Garam Masala

Equipment

Frying Pan
Sandwich toaster

How to prepare the recipe for the vegetable sandwich

1. To prepare the recipe for the vegetable sandwich, you first need to heat a frying pan and add oil into it.
2. Pour the cumin into it and wait for it to start spluttering.
3. Add the garlic and mix it well till you get the pleasant aroma that comes next.
4. You can then add the tomatoes and a little salt. To ensure the salt isn't too much, taste it as you sprinkle.
5. Cover the mix and allow it to cook softly for a while. Before allowing it to cook, you can add the red chili (if you have and want to use it).

How to prepare the vegetable sandwich

1. Spread the butter on one side of the bread slices and allow it to blend well.
2. Spread the vegetable mix on the inner side of the bread slices.
3. Cover it up with another slice of bread.
4. Put it into a sandwich toaster until you get your desired crispy look and taste.
5. Your vegetable sandwich is ready, and you can serve it hot.

PECAN PIE MINI MUFFIN

Serving: 24 pies
Baking Time: 25 minutes
Plus Cooling Time: 30 minutes

Ingredients

1 Cup of Packed Light Brown Sugar
1 Cup of Chopped Pecans
2 Large Eggs
24 Mini Muffin Liners
1 Teaspoon of Vanilla Extract
½ Cup of Melted Butter
¼ Teaspoon of Salt
½ Teaspoon of Baking Powder
½ Cup of All-purpose Flour

Equipment

Cooking Spray
Bowl
Mini Muffin Cups
Pan

1. Set your oven to a temperature of 425°F.
2. Line 24 mini muffin cups with liners and spray them lightly with a cooking spray.
3. Get a bowl and mix the flour, baking powder, brown sugar, and salt till you get your desired taste.
4. After you have done that, it's time to put your melted butter in the mix.
5. The vanilla extract and the eggs would come next, and then you blend the mix well till there is a proper combination of the ingredients.
6. Sprinkle the mix with the remaining ½ cup of chopped pecans.
7. Allow to bake for about ten to twelve minutes.
8. Remove from the pan when done, and allow to cool a little before serving.

SPOTTY MUFFINS

Serving: 12 People
Baking Time: 20 minutes
Plus Cooling Time: 30 minutes

Ingredients

1 Teaspoon of Baking Powder
300g of Flour
110g of Caster Sugar
150g of Colored Sweets
200ml of Milk
1 Teaspoon of Vanilla Extract
2 Eggs
Melted Butter (80g)

Equipment:

Bowl

Directions

1. Set your oven's temperature to 200°C.
2. Get a bowl and mix the flour, casted sugar, and baking powder.
3. Add half of the sweets and mix properly.
4. In another bowl, create a mix of the milk, vanilla extract, and eggs.
5. Stir properly till they all blend and mix well.
6. Add the melted butter to the mix and add the dry ingredients into the rest of the mix till there is an excellent blend.
7. Put the mix into cases and bake for about twenty minutes until it's ready.
8. You can remove them from the oven when they're ready and allow them to cool for some time before serving.

BAKED BEANS MUFFINS

Serving: 12 People
Baking Time: 20-25 minutes
Plus Cooling Time: 35 minutes

Ingredients

120ml of Full-Flat Milk
45g of Melted Butter
160g of Flour
½ Tablespoon of Baking Powder
1 Large Egg
220g Can Of Baked Beans in Tomato Sauce
60g of Well-grated Mature Cheddar

Equipment

Bowl
Tray

Directions

1. Get a bowl for mixing.
2. Ensure the bowl is microwave-acceptable so you can heat the butter inside it till it gets melted. After this is done, set it aside.
3. Now get the egg, melted butter, and milk mixture and pour it into the center of the flour.
4. Add the baked beans and then stir well till it mixes properly.
5. Next, add the grated cheese and keep mixing. When this is done, place them on a tray and into the hot oven. Allow the muffins to cook well for a couple of minutes (between twenty and twenty-five minutes is enough).
6. The baked breads will then rise to show that it is ready
7. Bring them out to cool before serving afterwards.

FRUITY BREAKFAST MUFFINS

Serving: 10 People
Baking Time: 25 minutes
Plus Cooling Time: 25 minutes

Ingredients

50g of Jumbo Oats
200g of Plain Wholemeal Flour
1.5 Teaspoon of Baking Powder
0.5 Teaspoon of Baking Soda
50g of Melted Coconut Oil
100g of Plain Yogurt
1 Medium-sized Egg
2 Tablespoons of Honey
2 Mashed Bananas
1 Teaspoon Of Vanilla Extract
2 Clemente's
80g of Blueberries

Equipment

Bowl
Muffin Cases

Directions

1. A temperature of 180°C is enough for your oven heating. In the oven, place ten muffin cases and move to the next step.
2. Next, in one bowl, mix the oats, flour, baking soda, and baking powder and stir well.
3. Then in another bowl, you mix the yogurt, egg, coconut oil, mashed banana, vanilla extract, and the honey. Make sure you mix well.
4. Combine the wet and dry ingredients till they mix up well, then add the blueberries, the Clemente's, and the juice.
5. When you have finished mixing, scoop the mix and pour into the muffin cases.
6. Place them in the oven to bake for about twenty-five minutes until you get your desired result.

MINI CHOCOLATE CHIP MUFFINS

Serving: 24 People
Baking Time: 10-12 minutes
Plus Cooling Time: 40 minutes

Ingredients

1 Large Egg
1 Teaspoon of Vanilla Extract
2 Teaspoons of Baking Powder
½ Cups of Flour (All-purpose)
½ Cup of Mini Chocolate Chips
½ Cup of Whole Milk
1/3 Cup of Vegetable Oil
¾ Cup of Granulated Sugar
½ Teaspoons of Salt

Equipment

Muffin Cups
Bowl

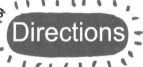

Directions

1. For this muffin, you can set your oven to a temperature of 375 Degree F
2. Mix the flour, salt, baking powder, and sugar all in a single bowl and stir till it becomes smooth.
3. Get another bowl and mix the vegetable oil, vanilla extract, egg, and milk, then stir as well. You would need to mix the wet and dry ingredients and then mix thoroughly till you attain some level of smoothness.
4. When that is done, pour the mix into your muffin cups adequately and bake for about twelve minutes.
5. After that, take it out for it to cool thoroughly before serving.

BLUEBERRY MUFFINS

Serving: 8 People

Ingredients

195g of Flour (All-purpose)
150g of Granulated Sugar (plus an extra Tablespoon for Muffin Tops)
2 Teaspoons of Baking Powder
1 Large Egg
¼ Teaspoon of Fine Sea Salt
80ml of Oil (Neutral Flavor)
1½ Teaspoons of Vanilla Extract
80-120ml of milk
6-8 Ounces of Fresh Blueberries

Equipment

Bowl
Muffin Cases
Muffin Cups

 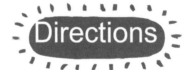

Directions

1. Allow your oven to heat for up to 400°F and line up your muffin cases with paper liners.
2. Next, mix the flour, sugar, salt, and baking powder in a bowl, then add oil, egg, milk, and the vanilla extract. Stir thoroughly.
3. Add the mixture with the dry ingredients in a fresh bowl and combine them well (you can use a fork). Remember not to over mix. When that is done, you can fold in the blueberries.
4. Now pour the mix into your muffin cups and bake for about twenty minutes.
5. When it's ready, bring it out and allow it to cool thoroughly.
6. Now you have your delicious Blueberry Muffins prepared to be eaten.

These are some of the best bread recipes out there that our young bakers can try. I'm sure you will enjoy them. They are not only delicious but also easy to prepare, as long as you follow instructions correctly

chapter three

YEAST BREAD RECIPES

FLOWERPOT BREAD

Serving: 6 people
Baking Time: 30 minutes
Plus Cooling Time: 3 hours

Ingredients

4 cups (512g) of all-purpose flour
2 cups of lukewarm water
2 teaspoons of sugar
2 teaspoons of yeast
Small quantity of butter
Sea salt for sprinkling

Equipment

Six small flowerpots
A bowl
A knife

  Directions

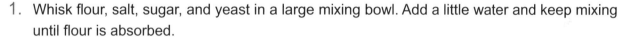

1. Whisk flour, salt, sugar, and yeast in a large mixing bowl. Add a little water and keep mixing until flour is absorbed.
2. Cover the bowl containing the mixture with a towel. Put it in a warm place and leave it to rise. This can take two hours.
3. Preheat the oven to 4250F.
4. Rub the inside of the flowerpots with butter. A tablespoon of butter should do.
5. Carefully put the dough in the flowerpots.
6. Bake for 15 minutes.
7. Reduce the heat to 3750 and leave it for another 15 minutes.
8. Run a toothpick through the dough to check if it non-sticky.
9. Once the toothpick is non-sticky, run a knife around the edge of each flower pot and turn each out to a cooling tray to cool for 20 minutes.

Your flowerpot bread is ready! You know what kiddies? You can tie a bow around it and return it to the flowerpot with some beautiful flowers near it, to give as gift or to take nice pictures with.

CHEESY GARLIC BREAD

Serving: 2 people
Baking Time: 16 minutes
Plus Cooling Time: 25 minutes

Ingredients

1 French or Italian bread – slice bread in half equal length
¼ cup of softened cooking butter
1 tablespoon Fresh parsley
2 tablespoons of Olive oil
Salt and pepper
1 cup and a quarter of shredded mozzarella cheese
1/3 Shredded Parmesan cheese
Fresh granulated garlic

Equipment:

Bowl

1. Preheat oven to 400oF
2. Mix butter, olive oil, garlic, pepper and salt in a bowl.
3. Spread the mixture over the inner part of both breads and wrap foil gently over the bread.
4. Bake for 10 minutes.
5. After removing bread from the oven, sprinkle it with cheese and allow it to bake again till it is golden. This should take 5 to 6 minutes.
6. Sprinkle the top of your bread with parsley. You can cut it into slices and serve it warm.

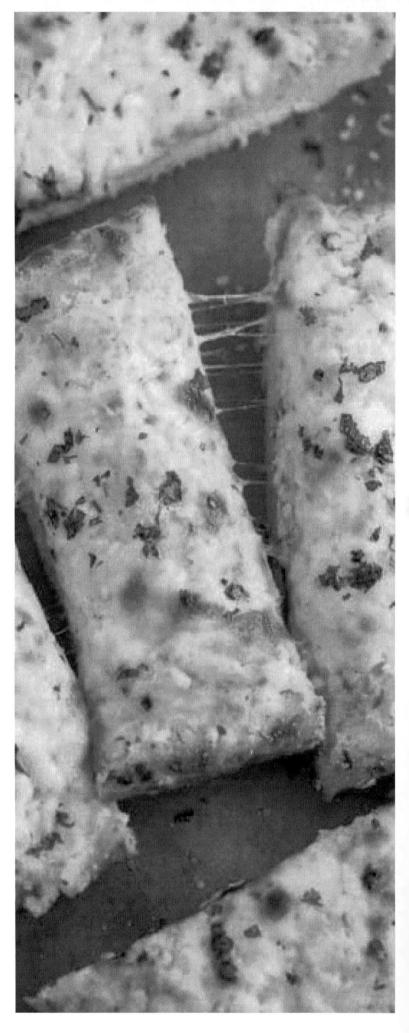

CUDDLY EGG MEN

Serving: 4 people
Baking Time: 16 minutes
Plus Cooling Time: 1 hour 60minutes

Ingredients

400 grams of white flour
½ tablespoon of salt
7grams sachet of dried yeast
2 tablespoon olive oil
4 big eggs

Equipment

Baking sheets
Scissors
Skewer
Knife
Bowl

 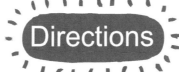

Directions

1. Stir the flour, salt, sugar and yeast.
2. Add 250ml of water and oil, then mix to soft dough. A little water can be added if the mixture is not satisfying.
3. Keep kneading dough until it is smooth and then put the mixture in a bowl.
4. Cover the mixture and leave it in a warm place to rise. This can take an hour.
5. Preheat the oven to 200°C and knead the dough again. Cut it into four.
6. Get ready for some creativity here. Mold a little part of the dough into a round object like a head.
7. Shape other pieces into straight rolls. These pieces should look like sausages.
8. Now, attach the head like shape you created earlier to the rolls of sausages using cold water. Be careful not to use too much water. This is the dough man. The straight rolls are his arms.
9. Place an egg on the dough man's tummy.
10. Fold the attached arms over the egg and use cold water to make it stay.
11. The eyes are missing! So, use a wooden skewer to make the dough man see.
12. Do the same with the remaining dough men and leave them for about 10 minutes.
13. Bake each dough men in the oven for 20 minutes until it is well risen and golden in color.
14. After it is cool for a few minutes, peel the egg and eat it with your dough man.

HEDGEHOG ROLLS

Serving: 6 people
Baking Time: 15 minutes
Plus Cooling Time: 2 hours

Ingredients

500 grams brown bread mix
with pack
25 grams salted butter
Flour for dusting
12 raisins
6 flaked almonds

Equipment

Rolling pin
Stand mixer (for mixing the dough)

 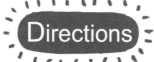

1. Follow the instructions on the pack to make the bread mixture with butter.
2. Let the dough rest for 5 minutes, and then knead for five minutes.
3. Divide the dough into six pieces.
4. Sprinkle some flour all over the surface of the pan, and roll a little portion of your dough in between your hands making them into balls.
5. Now, make the balls into a hedgehog shape by pulling a part of your ball out a little in a way that makes it look like a snout. Remember how the noses of animals like sea lions and pigs project outwards? Yeah, that's right. Make your balls look just like that.
6. Add a flaked almond at the end of the snouts.
7. Put the mixture in a baking sheet and cover it with a towel to rise.
8. Heat the oven to 200C.
9. Use a scissors to carefully form spikes that are meant to be at the back of your hedgehog.
10. Put your raisins in to form the eye
11. Take a look at this diagram and try to make sure yours looks like this.
12. Bake for 15 minutes

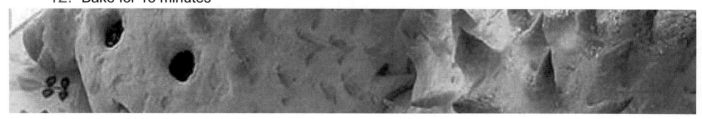

LAZY WOMAN BREAD

Serving: 5 people
Baking Time: 20 minutes
Plus Cooling Time: 2 hours 30 minutes

Equipment:

a container

Ingredients

Six cups of warm water
½ cup of oil
¼ cup of sugar
¼ cup of yeast
¼ cup of powdered milk
7 cups of white flour
5 cups of fun grains (red wheat, graham, potato flakes, oatmeal and anything you want to add)
1 tablespoon of salt

Directions

1. Mix flour, sugar, yeast powdered milk, olive oil and fun grains together and add water. It is indeed a lazy woman bread! There is less stress in it.
2. Allow the mixture to rise for an hour or two, and then put it in a fridge.
3. You can allow the bread stay for thirty minutes before baking in order to reactivate the yeast.
4. Bake until it is done.

PIZZA DOUGH SCIENCE

Serving: 3 people

Baking Time: 1 hour

Plus Cooling Time: 1 hour

Ingredients

4 cups of unbleached all-purpose flour

2 tablespoon of Olive Oil

1 teaspoon of sugar

2 teaspoons of salt

1 and 1/3 cups of warm water

2 ¼ teaspoons yeast

Equipment:

Bowl

 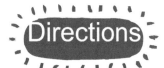

Directions

1. Mix all the dry ingredients together. These are the flour, yeast, salt and sugar.
2. Add the oil to the mixture. Mix properly.
3. Add warm water.
4. When all the ingredients are properly mixed, the yeast will start to break down the sugar. In doing this, it gives off carbon dioxide. This reaction is what makes dough rise.
5. Roll your dough into balls with your hands. Make sure that the dough is tight and does not be crack.
6. Oil a pan and place the dough in it. Then, cover it with a towel or wax paper.
7. Allow it to stay at room temperature till the size doubles.
8. Place the dough in a fridge to slow down the yeast's activity.
9. If your dough is well made, you can use it for three to five days.

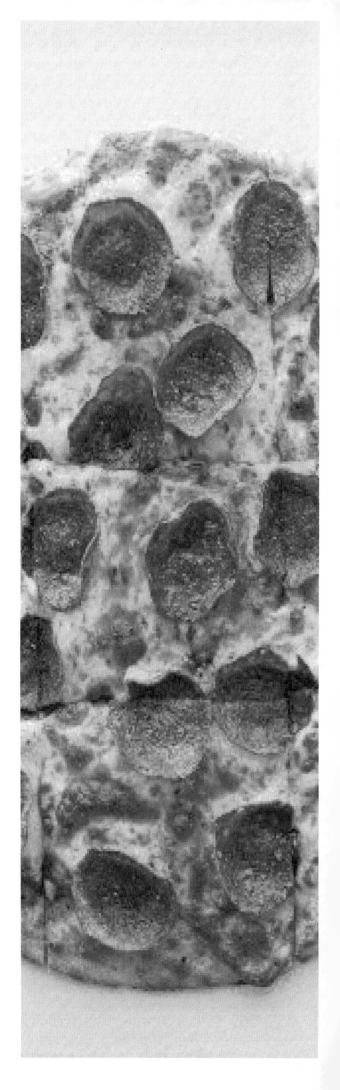

FRIENDSHIP BREAD (Armish)

Serving: 2 loaves or 18 slices
Baking Time: 1 hour
Plus Cooling Time: 1 hour 20 minutes

Ingredients

1 cup Armish friendship bread starter

This starter is the reason behind the name friendship bread. This means you cannot make the bread without starting with a part of the bread made by someone else. And what is friendship without sharing?

1 cup of oil
½ cup of milk
3 eggs
1 cup of sugar
½ cup of vanilla
2 teaspoons of cinnamon
2 cups of flour
1 and ½ teaspoon of baking powder
½ teaspoon of salt
½ teaspoon of baking soda
1 box of vanilla instant pudding (small box)
1 cup of chopped nuts (optional)
1 cup of raisins (optional)

Equipment:

Loaf Pan
Bowl

 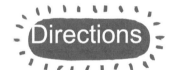

1. Preheat oven to 3250F.
2. Mix all the ingredients listed above in a large mixing bowl.
3. Grease your loaf pans and dust them with a mixture of 1 and ½ teaspoon of cinnamon and ½ cup of sugar.
4. Pour the mixture into the pans and sprinkle the remaining sugar and vanilla on the top. Bake for an hour until a toothpick put into it can come out clean.
5. There, your friendship bread is ready!

Ingredients

4 cups white bread flour (set aside a few tablespoons)
1 tablespoon of instant yeast
2 tablespoons of softened butter
3 tablespoons of melted butter to spread on the top of the bread when made
2 tablespoons of sugar
1 and 1/2 cups of warm water
Pinch of salt and 1 tablespoon of sea salt to sprinkle after baking

Equipment

Large mixing bowl
Sieve
Pastry brush
Scissors
Baking tray
Wire rack

LITTLE RED HEN BREAD

Serving: 3 People
Baking: 20 minutes
Plus Cooling Time: 20 minutes

Directions

1. Put warm water, sugar, and yeast in a mixing bowl.
2. Allow it to rest for about 5 minutes.
3. Add 2 cups of flour gradually into the bowl.
4. Add butter and salt and mix gently until dough cleanly pulls away from the bowl without being sticky.
5. Knead the dough till it is smooth for about 5 minutes.
6. Then, cover the bowl with a clean towel.
7. Put it in a warm place and leave to rise for 30 minutes or more, till the dough is almost double.
8. Put your dough on a floured surface and divide it into two equal parts.
9. Grease your pan and take one part of the dough to form a snake shape as seen in the picture below.
10. Cut it into twelve pieces and roll each of them into a ball.
11. Do the same for the other half and place it in your pan.
12. Rub the melted butter on the dough.
13. Preheat the oven to 4000 F.
14. Sprinkle sea salt on each roll and leave it to rise again.
15. Bake for 15 minutes until rolls are golden.
16. Enjoy your bread with the remaining butter.

BEER BREAD

Serving: 6 to 8 people
Baking Time: 1 hour 3 minutes
Plus Cooling Time: 1 hour 30 minutes

Ingredients

3 cups of sifted flour
3 teaspoons of baking powder
There is no need for this if the flour can rise by itself. Ask mummy to show you the difference.
1 teaspoon of salt (like the baking powder, there is no need for this if the flour is self-rising)
¼ cup of sugar
1 (12 ounce) can beer
¼ cup of melted butter

Equipment

Sieve

1. Make sure you sift your flour.
2. Preheat the oven to 375 degrees.
3. Mix all your dry ingredients (flour, baking powder, salt, sugar) and add your beer.
4. Grease your pan and pour the mixture in.
5. Pour melted butter on your dough and bake for 1 hour.
6. Allow it to cool for 15 minutes.

HOMEMADE PRETZELS

Serving: 48 people
Baking Time: 40 minutes
Plus Cooling Time: 1 hour 40 minutes

Ingredients

1 ½ cups of water
1 tablespoon salt
1 packet of dry yeast
4 1/2 cups of flour
3 tablespoons of oil
2/3 cup of baking soda
2 beaten eggs
Coarse salt

Equipment:

Plastic wrap

 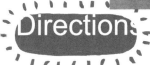

Directions

1. Mix salt, sugar, water and yeast together and allow it rest for 5minutes till yeast foams.
2. Add flour and oil and mix till dough is well formed
3. Rub the dough in a little oil and cover it with a plastic wrap or towel for 1 hour. Put this in a warm place.
4. Preheat oven to 450 degrees
5. Cut dough into 8 pieces and form thin ropes with them.
6. Twist the two ends to form a pretzel shape.
7. Boil baking soda in a large pot of water and boil each piece for 30 seconds per side.
8. Transfer your pretzels to a baking sheet and brush it with egg wash.
9. Sprinkle with salt.
10. Bake for 15 minutes till it becomes golden brown.

FRENCH BREAD

Serving: 30 minutes
Baking Time: 40 minutes
Plus Cooling Time: 1 hour 40 minutes

Ingredients

6 cups of all-purpose flour
2 cups of warm water
2 ½ packs active dry yeast

1 tablespoon cornmeal
1 teaspoon of salt
1 egg white
1 tablespoon of water

Equipment

Wooden spoon
Stand mixer
Sharp knife

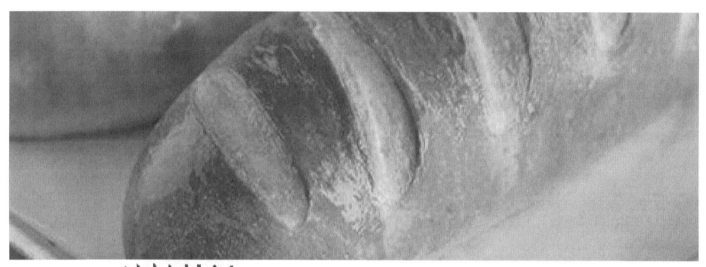

1. Mix the flour, yeast and salt in 2 cups of warm water, and beat until it is well blended with a stand mixer.
2. Use a wooden spoon to stir in the flour.
3. Lightly flour a surface and knead the flour to make stiff dough that is smooth.
4. Do this for about 8 to 10 minutes.
5. Shape into a ball and place the dough in a greased bowl. Turn it over once.
6. Cover with towel, and allow it rise in a warm place until the dough is double.
7. Punch the dough and divide it into half.
8. Put the mixture in a floured surface.
9. Cover and leave it for 10 minutes.
10. Roll each part into a large rectangle.
11. Roll the triangle up by starting from a long side.
12. Put little water at the edge and seal the triangle.
13. Grease a large baking sheet.
14. Sprinkle cornmeal on a baking sheet already greased.
15. Put your loaves on the baking sheet.
16. Brush the mixture with egg and cover with a wet towel.
17. Allow it to rise until it is doubled. Leave for 40 minutes.
18. Use a sharp knife to make 3 or 4 diagonal cuts about 1/4 inches deep across top of each loaf.
19. Preheat the oven to 375°F for 20 minutes.
20. Brush the mixture again with egg white mixture.
21. Bake for another 20 minutes until bread is done.
22. Remove the baked bread and leave to cool on a wire rack.

WHOLE WHEAT BREAD

Serving: 36 people
Baking Time: 30 minutes
Plus Cooling Time: 3 hours

Ingredients

3 cups of warm water
2 packs of active dry yeast
1/3 cup honey
5 cups bread flour
1 tablespoon of salt
5 tablespoons melted butter
3 ½ cups whole wheat flour
2 tablespoons melted butter (for brushing)

Equipment:

Towel

 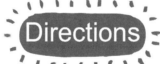

1. Mix warm water, yeast, and ½ cup of honey, in a large bowl.
2. Add 5 cups of white flour, and stir. Leave to rest for 30 minutes.
3. Mix 3 tablespoons of butter with 1/3 of cup honey, and salt.
4. Mix the wheat flour in the mixture and flour the surface for kneading.
5. Knead the flour till it is non-sticky.
6. Add additional 2 cups of wheat flour.
7. Grease your bowl, turning the dough to be covered by it.
8. Cover with a towel and allow it rise in a warm place until doubled.
9. Punch down, and divide into three loaves of bread.
10. Place in greased pans, and allow the dough to rise.
11. Bake at 350°F for 30 minutes and try not to over bake.
12. Brush the tops of the loaves with 2 tablespoons of melted butter when done to prevent crust from getting hard.
13. Cool completely.

REFRIGERAT OR ROLLS

Serving: 8 people
Baking Time: 15 minutes
Plus Cooling Time: 1 hour 40 minutes

Ingredients

2 cups of hot water
½ cup of sugar
½ cup vegetable shortening
1 tablespoon of salt
2 packs of dry yeast in water
2 beaten eggs
7 cups of flour

Equipment

Smooth board for kneading
Muffin tins

 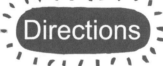

Directions

1. Put yeast in half cup of warm water and leave for 15 minutes
2. In another bowl, add shortening and hot water.
3. Add sugar and salt.
4. After the mixture is cool, continue to stir and add flour until it is soft.
5. Knead the mixture on a floured board until it is smooth.
6. Oil a bowl and leave your mixture in it.
7. Keep turning the dough in the bowl so that it will be covered in oil.
8. Cover with a lid and refrigerate it overnight.
9. When ready to bake, cut dough into 3 equal parts and cut the parts into smaller pieces.
10. Roll the pieces into balls.
11. Place each piece into a muffin tin and brush with melted butter.
12. Leave it to rise till it is double sized.
13. Bake it at 350°F for 20 minutes or until it is golden.
14. Brush again with butter and serve.
15. Grease your baking pan and sprinkle with corn meal.
16. Put your dough in it and brush with the egg white.
17. Cover it up to rise again for 40 minutes.

BANNOK

Serving: 12
Baking Time: 40 minutes
Plus Cooling Time: 60 minutes

Ingredients

3 cups all-purpose flour
1 tablespoon salt
1 teaspoons baking powder
¼ cup of melted cooking butter
1 1/2 cup water

Equipment:

Fork, bowl

1. Mix the flour, salt and baking powder together in a bowl.
2. Add the melted butter and water to the flour mixture.
3. Use a fork to stir to make it into a ball shape.
4. Knead your dough gently on a lightly floured surface.
5. Make sure you make it into a small circle which is about 1 inch thick. You can cut it in twelve places.
6. Grease your frying pan and cook your dough over a medium heat.
7. Allow each side to cook for about 15 minutes before turning. You can use two lifters to turn your mixture easil

BREAD CLAY BEADS

Instructions: This bread is not for food. It is a craft.

Serving: 2 People

Baking Time: 40 minutes

Plus Cooling Time: 1 – 2 hours (or all through the night)

Ingredients

*   White bread
*   Glue
*   Paint

Equipment

*   Spoon
*   Bowl
*   Plastic
*   Caps
*   Clay cutter

1. Remove the tough outer part of the loaf of bread – the crust.
2. Tear the bread into small pieces.
3. Add glue to the bread in bits as you mix with a spoon and then your hand.

This can get messy but the result would be worth it.

4. Continue to knead until the clay becomes smooth and flexible. Your mixture would turn into a ball as you mix.
5. Add more glue if the clay is not coming together as a perfect ball.
6. Lemon can be added to give it a nice smell. A few drops of paint can be added to the mixture if you desire colored clay.
7. To get your bead, roll out the dough to be slightly thick.
8. Use drinking straw, clay cutters or plastic caps to cut your clay into beads like the ones in the picture.
9. Leave the beads to dry in a warm place for few hours or throughout the night.
10. You can put a rope or fishing line in between the beads to form a round chain-like bead. It is now your bead, be creative about what you do with it. You can store the bread clay beads in a zipper sandwich b

CHAPTER FOUR

PIZZA, FLATBREAD AND OTHER SAVORY BAKED GOODS

SAVORY BEEF HAMANTASCHEN

Serving: 7 people
Baking Time: 25 minutes
Plus Cooling Time: 3 hours

Ingredients

Dough
2 tablespoons of dry yeast
1 cup and 2 tablespoons of warm water
Pinch of sugar
3 1/2 cups bread flour
Pinch of salt
1 tablespoon of olive oil
1 big egg

Filling

2 tablespoons olive oil
1 onion (already diced)
1 pound of ground sirloin
2 tablespoons dried mint
1 tablespoon each allspice, cinnamon and paprika
1/2 tablespoon ground cloves
Pinch of cayenne
1/2 cup pine nuts
1/2 cup golden raisins
Yogurt sauce
4 cloves of minced garlic
Juice of two lemons
Pinch of salt
2 cups of plain Greek yogurt
2 tablespoons dried mint

Equipment

Bowl
Baking sheet
Parchment paper

 **Directions**

1. Preheat oven to 350Degree F
2. Prepare the dough by mixing flour, salt, oil, yeast and egg in a large bowl.
3. Knead for ten minutes until dough is smooth.
4. Place dough in well-oiled bowl and cover.
5. Put in a warm place to rise until doubled.

For the filling

1. Heat the olive oil over medium heat.
2. Fry the onions for 5 minutes till it is soft.
3. Add salt and pepper to taste.
4. Add ground beef and spices and cook till the meat is no longer pink.
5. Add pine nuts and raisins
6. Leave until the pine nuts are toasted.
7. After your dough rises, divide into it into four pieces.
8. Take one piece and roll it out as thinly as possible on a lightly floured board.
9. Cut dough into 6-7 rounds.
10. Fold in two sides of the circle, using two hands and pinch together.
11. Pinch all three corners together after folding the bottom side.
12. Close the pastries properly.
13. Line a baking sheet with parchment paper.
14. Place the filled pastries on the baking sheet.
15. Brush pastries with egg wash.
16. Bake pastries for 25 minutes and cool on a wire rac

To make the yogurt sauce

1. Add lemon juice and salt to minced garlic and leave it for five minutes.
2. Combine garlic mixture with the Greek yogurt and mint.
3. Season with salt and pepper.
4. Add your extra virgin olive oi

RED LENTIL BANANA BREAD

Serving: 12 muffins
Baking Time: 20 minutes
Plus Cooling Time: 1 hour

Ingredients

1 cup cooked green lentils
3/4 cup mashed banana
1/4 cup oil
1 egg
1/4 cups of sugar
1 tablespoon vanilla
2/3 cup oats
2/3 cup white whole wheat flour
1 tablespoon baking soda
1 tablespoon cinnamon
1/2 cup chocolate chips

Equipment

Food processor
Muffin tins

1. Heat oven to 375 degrees
2. Put cooked lentils and oil in a food processor and make to be smooth.
3. Add mashed banana, sugar, egg and vanilla and process the mixture again.
4. Put flour, baking soda, oats and cinnamon in the processor, and process until it is evenly mixed.
5. It is time to add chocolate chips.
6. Quite simple to make right?
7. Grease the muffin tins and bake at 3750 for 20 minutes or until toothpick comes out clean.

SAVORY BAKED PUMPKIN PASTRIES

Serving: 4
Baking Time: 30 minutes
Plus Cooling Time: 1 hour

Ingredients

Sugar
Pumpkin
Olive oil

Seasonings:

Kosher salt
Chili powder
Garlic

Preparation:

Put all seasoning in the pumpkin and
roast it until it is tender.
Equipment: Vegetable Peeler

1. Soften the pumpkin in the microwave, and then cut it in half.
2. Remove the pulp and seeds.
3. Cut each pumpkin half into four moon shaped slices.
4. Peel the skin off with a vegetable peeler.
5. Cut the pumpkin slices into cubes.
6. Put the sliced cubes on the baking sheet and coat them with olive
   oil and spices. Bake for 30 minutes at 425 Degree F

STONE FRUIT BLUEBERRY PIE

Serving: 6 people
Baking Time: 1 hour
Plus cooling time: 4 hours

Ingredients

8 ounces cold, unsalted European-style butter
2 1/2 cups all-purpose flour
1 tablespoon sugar
2 teaspoons salt
½ cup ice water
1 tablespoon lemon juice or vinegar
Filling
1 tablespoon each of flour and sugar mixed
(to line bottom crust)
3 cups blueberries
3 cups sliced nectarines or peaches
1/4 cup sugar
Zest and juice of 1/2 lemon
3 tablespoon tapioca starch
1/2 tablespoon each allspice and ground cloves
Dash cocktail bitters (optional)

Topping

1 egg beaten
Demerara or Turbinado sugar for sprinkling

Equipment

Rolling pin
Pastry board
Pie plate
Food processor
Tin foil

Directions

This is quite a long one. With patience, you would get it.

1. Cut butter into small cubes and place in the refrigerator. Mix the flour, salt and sugar in the bowl of a food processor and pulse a few times. Add the refrigerated ingredients to the dry ingredients and process.
2. Mix lemon juice or vinegar together with ice water. Then put six tablespoons of the mixture in the food processor. Keep pulsing until well combined. Put the dough in a well-floured board.
3. Knead the dough till a ball is formed. Put your dough in a plastic bag after dividing it into two. Keep it in the refrigerator overnight. Use rolling pin to flatten the dough before rolling it out, so it will become softer.
4. Heat oven to 425 degrees and grease the pie plate. Dust a pastry board and rolling pin with flour.
5. Roll the dough out and mix properly. Now, put your pie dough at the center of the plate and press it into the bottom and sides. Fold over any excess dough at the edges.
6. Sprinkle the bottom of the plate with the sugar and flour mix. Leave the dough in the pie plate for 30 minutes.

To make the filling

Add the blueberries, sugar, nectarines, tapioca starch, lemon zest and juice, spices and bitters, in a large bowl. Set the mixture aside to allow the sugar and lemon juice to draw out the berries' juice.

To prepare the lattice top

1. Roll out the second dough ball like above.
2. Use a paring knife to cut equal strips of dough about 1/2 to 3/4 inch thick.
3. Put the filling on top of the bottom crust.
4. Lay out strips of dough horizontally to create a lattice top.
5. Lay down one vertical strip and fold back every other strip. Then, unfold the dough strips.
6. It is time to fold back the strips that was not folded the first time and lay a second layer of vertical strip.
7. Unfold and repeat this with the remaining strips of dough to create a woven lattice.
8. After trimming, crimp together the edges of the bottom and top crusts.
9. Mix the egg with one tablespoon of water and beat together.
10. Brush the top with egg wash and brush the edges also.
11. Sprinkle with the Turbinado or Demerera sugar. Bake for 20-25 minutes till it is golden brown.To prevent them from burning, cover the edges with tin foil.
12. Reduce the heat to 375 degrees and bake for another 30-35 minutes till you see the filling bubbling.
13. Cool on a rack completely (for several hours) before slicing to allow filling to set

FIG HONEY GALETTE

Serving: 8 people
Baking Time: 40 minutes
Plus Cooling Time: 3 hours 40 minutes

Ingredients

½ cup whole wheat flour
1 ¼ cups all-purpose flour
White sugar
1 teaspoon salt
1 ½ sticks cold unsalted butter, cubed
¼ cup ice water
1 tablespoon lemon juice

Topping

1 container mascarpone cheese
1 egg yolk
1 tablespoon milk
2 pints fresh figs, halved
2 tablespoons of honey
1½ teaspoons vanilla extract

Equipment

Food processor
Parchment paper

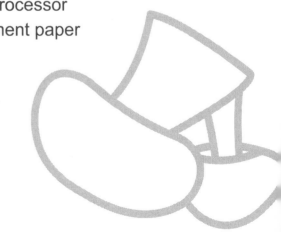

Directions

1. Mix flour, salt and sugar in a food processor.
2. Add butter and mix until it is crumbly.
3. Add lemon juice and water. Beat a few more times.
4. Put dough in a large bowl and gently knead till it forms well.
5. Wrap mixture in plastic wrap and refrigerate for 1 hour.
6. After you unwrap the dough, allow it to stay for 5 to 10 minutes.
7. Roll the dough on a floured piece of parchment paper till it is 1/4-inch thick.
8. Place the parchment with the dough onto a baking sheet.
9. Stir the mascarpone until it is soft.
10. Stir it in egg yolk, vanilla and honey.
11. Leaving a 2-inch border spread some more dough.
12. Top with your figs in a circular motion.
13. Fold the dough edges over the fruit while using parchment to help lift the edges.
14. You can pleat it the way you want.
15. Leave the fruit to be exposed in the center.
16. Make it chill and cover for 1 hour
17. Preheat the oven to 375 degrees
18. Brush edges with milk.
19. Sprinkle the galette with turbinado sugar
20. Bake until crust is golden and the filling is bubbly for 40 to 45 minutes.
21. Leave it to cool for 30 minutes.

APPLE STREUSEL TART

Serving: 6 people
Baking Time: 1 hour
Plus Cooling Time: 2hours

Ingredients

1½ cups cake flour (not self-rising)
½ teaspoon baking powder
3 tablespoons cold cream cheese (cut into small pieces)
5 tablespoons of unsalted butter
2 to 3 tablespoon of ice water
2 teaspoons fresh lemon juice
1 cup of brown sugar
2 tablespoons of all-purpose flour
1 teaspoon of Chinese five spice powder
¼ teaspoon of salt
6 large Granny Smith apples (peeled, cored and sliced -about 6 cups)

Equipment

Fork
Food processor
Wax paper
Tart pan with a removable bottom

Directions

1. Heat oven to 425°F.
2. Add cake flour, salt and baking powder in a food processor and beat until well blended.
3. Add your butter and cream cheese.
4. Beat the butter and cheese 15 times till mixture resembles coarse crumbs.
5. Put mixture in a mixing bowl.
6. In another bowl, stir together 2 tablespoons of lemon juice and ice water.
7. Add this mixture to the dry ingredients and mix with a fork.
8. Dough should be dry and crumbly but should be able to hold together when you pinch a small amount between your fingers.
9. Form a ball with the dough and flatten it into a 4-inch disk.
10. Roll out pastry between 2 sheets of wax paper and put it into a fluted tart pan with a removable bottom, gently putting it into the pan.
11. Refrigerate until you want to use it.

To make your filling

1. Mix flour, five-spice powder, salt and brown sugar in a large bowl.
2. Add toss and apple to coat well.
3. Spread the apples evenly in tart shell.

For your streusel topping

1. Stir sugar, butter and flour with a fork in a small bowl until crumbly.
2. Sprinkle over apples.
3. Bake for 50 to 60 minutes or until apples are tender when a fork goes into it, and crust and topping are brown.
4. Leave to coo

PIZZA PRETZELS

Serving: 4 People
Baking Time: 30 minutes
Plus Cooling Time: 1 hour 30 minutes

Ingredients

1 tablespoon cornmeal
1 tablespoon Virgin Olive Oil
1 tablespoon all Purpose Flour
1 Cup tomato pasta sauce (heated)
1 can Pillsbury™ refrigerated classic pizza crust
28 slices pepperoni
4 teaspoons of grated Parmesan cheese
8 pieces mozzarella string cheese

Equipment

Cookie Sheet

Directions

1. Preheat oven to 425°F.
2. Brush cookie sheet with 1/2 tablespoon of oil.
3. Sprinkle cornmeal on your cookie sheet.
4. Sprinkle flour over a smooth surface.
5. On the floured surface, unroll pizza crust dough by starting at the center.
6. Press dough into 16 x 10-inch rectangle.
7. With knife or pizza cutter cut the dough into 4 strips.
8. Place 7 pepperoni slices equally on each dough strip, leaving a little part of each end uncovered.
9. Cut each string in half.
10. Place 4 halves of the cheese on pepperoni on each dough strip. Let each of the ends be unequal so it will fit.
11. Place the dough over the pepperoni and cheese, and tightly pinch it together.
12. Gently roll and shape into 16-inches logs.
13. Form each log into U-shape, then cross the ends and fold dough over so ends rest on bottom   of U-shape.
14. Place pretzels on cookie sheet.
15. Brush pretzels with remaining 1/2 tablespoon oil
16. Sprinkle with Parmesan cheese.
17. Bake mixture for 16 minutes or till pretzels are golden.
18. Serve with pasta sauce for dipping.

CHAPTER FIVE

COOKIES AND BARS

Chocolate chip Cookie Cones

Serving: 18 people

Baking Time: 8 minutes

Plus Cooling Time: 38 minutes

Ingredients

2 1/3 of all-purpose flour (291 gram)

1 teaspoon of baking soda

1 teaspoon of salt

1 cup of butter, softened (230 gram)

2/3 cup of granulated sugar (133 gram)

¾ cup of packed brown sugar (150 gram)

1 ½ teaspoons of vanilla extract

2 large eggs

1 ½ cups of mini-chocolate chips (262 gram)

Equipment

Measuring spoons and cups

Mixing bowls

Rubber spatula

Hand mixer

Baking sheet

Parchment paper

Ice cream cold mold

Directions

1. First heat the oven to 176°C. Then mix the flour, baking soda and salt in a small bowl.
2. Mix butter, granulated sugar, brown sugar and vanilla extract (that has good fragrance) in a large mixer bowl until it turns creamy.
3. Add eggs and mix well then add the flour mixture and mix until it blends.
4. Stir in mini chocolate chips.
5. Place ½ cup of batter on a silpat mat of a cookie sheet (for smaller cones use 1/2 cup)
6. Spread batter out to a 6 inch circle (or 5), let it be spacious.
7. Put it in the oven and bake for 9 minutes, then bring it out and let it cool for 2 minutes but don't allow it to get cold before using parchment paper.
8. Flip the cookie over so that it doesn't get hard.
9. Take an ice cream cold mold covered in parchment paper and roll it up.
10. Allow the parchment paper to hold the cookies squarely.
11. Allow the parchment paper with the cone to mold for 15 minutes.
12. Then add your ice cream.

HEART SHAPED COOKIES

Serving: 20 people
Baking Time: 8-10 minutes
Plus Cooling Time: 1 hour 40 minutes

Ingredients

3 cups of all-purpose flour
1 teaspoon baking powder
½ teaspoon salt
1 cup (2 sticks) butter, softened
1 cup of granulated sugar
1 large egg
1 teaspoon pure vanilla extract
1 teaspoon milk

For the Buttercream

1 (8-ozee) block cream cheese, softened
½ cup (1 stick) butter, softened
4 cup powdered sugar
1 teaspoon pure vanilla extract
¼ teaspoon salt
Pink and red food coloring and sprinkles

Equipment

Measuring spoons and cups
Mixing bowls
3 inch open-heart shaped cookie cutter
Parchment paper
Hand mixer
Offset spatula

Directions

1. In a bowl, stir cookie mix, flour, butter and egg until well blended and roll into 1 1/4-inch balls.Shape into a disk and wrap in plastic. Refrigerate 1 hour. Heat oven to 176°C.
2. Apply cooking spray on cookie cutter let it stick
3. Place on ungreased cookie sheet.
4. Apply pressure on dough ball evenly into cutter.
5. Remove cutter. Adjust the shape of dough if necessary.
6. Carry on the process of making heart-shaped cookies, placing them 2 inches apart on cookie sheet.
7. Spray cookie cutter as needed with cooking spray.
8. Allow it to bake for 6 to 8 minutes and cool 2 minutes
9. Remove from cookie shee

WOOKIE COOKIES

Serving: 20 people
Baking Time: 10 minutes
Plus Cooling Time: 3 hours 20 minutes

Ingredients

2¼ cups all-purpose flour
1 teaspoon baking soda
1 teaspoon salt
1 teaspoon ground cinnamon
1 cup unsalted butter
1 cup packed brown sugar
½ cup granulated sugar
2 large eggs
1½ teaspoons vanilla extract
1 cup milk chocolate chips
1 cup semi-sweet chocolate chips

Equipment

Measuring spoons and cups
Mixing bowls
3 inch human shaped cookie cutter
Parchment paper

Directions

1. Chill for at least 4 hours or overnight.
2. Dust a smooth surface with flour, and roll out a section of the dough to about ¼ inch or 6 millimeters thick.
3. Use a gingerbread man cookie cutter, or a knife to slice out your Wookies.
4. Wookies are tall, so you may want to stretch out the head and feet!
5. Line a baking sheet with parchment paper.
6. Place your wookies on the parchment paper, and score the cookie's surface to look like fur.
7. Bake at 180°C for 10 minutes. Your Wookies will puff up quickly.
8. Melt the white chocolate and the semi-sweet chocolate chips separately.
9. Allow chocolate to set completely before serving.
10. Add the bandolier, eyes and nose and serve the soft Wookie cooki

FUDGY MINT COOKIES

Serving: 36 people
Baking Time: 9 minutes
Plus Cooling Time: 1 hour 20 minutes

Ingredients

1 package devil's food cake mix (regular size)
½ cup butter, softened
2 large eggs, room temperature
1 tablespoon water
2 tablespoons powdered/confectioners' sugar
2 packages (5 ounces each) chocolate-covered thin mints

Equipment

Kitchen aid mixer
Measuring spoon and cup
Mixing bowl

1. Allow the oven to heat for a while at 180°C.
2. Use a kitchen aid mixer to combine your cake mix, butter, eggs and water to form a soft dough.
3. Refrigerate the dough by allowing it to be a little bit stronger. Then roll into balls and add your powdered/confectioners' sugar.
4. Place on cookie sheet and refrigerate a little longer. This will keep the dough from spreading out.
5. Bake for 9 minutes. Immediately press a mint into the center of each cookie.
6. Allow to cool for 2 minutes.
7. Remove from pan to wire racks to cool more.
8. Your fudgy mint cookies is ready to serv

BATTER COOKIES

Serving: 32 people
Baking Time: 14 minutes
Plus Cooling Time: 1 hour 25 minutes

Ingredients

2 sticks butter, softened
1 ¼ cups granulated sugar
¾ cup dark brown sugar
1 ounce unsweetened baking chocolate (melted)
3 large eggs, at room temperature
2 ½ cups all-purpose flour
½ cup unsweetened cocoa powder
1 ¼ teaspoons baking powder
1 ¼ teaspoons salt
1 tablespoon vanilla extract
1 ½ cups semisweet chocolate chi

Equipment

Parchment paper
Stand mixer
Measuring spoon and cup
Baking she

Directions

1. Allow the oven to heat for a while at 180°C.
2. Line a large baking sheet with parchment paper.
3. In a stand mixer with the beater blade attachment, beat the butter, granulated sugar, brown sugar and chocolate until smooth.
4. Add the eggs and mix until fully combined.
5. Sift together the flour, cocoa powder, baking powder and salt in a bowl and add slowly to the batter until mixed.
6. Add the vanilla and fold in the chocolate chips.
7. Apply a spoonful in the prepared baking sheet, about 2 inches apart. Bake for 14 minutes until it turns brown at the edges and is still soft. It should be slightly under-baked in the center.
8. Remove from the oven and allow to keep cooking on the cookie sheet for another 4 minutes.
9. While on the cookie sheet, add more chocolate chips just to make the cookies look more beautiful

PEANUT BUTTER COOKIES

Serving: 24 people
Baking Time: 15 minutes
Plus Cooling Time: 45 minutes

Ingredients

1 cup sugar (¼ cup additional to roll cookies)
1 stick butter, at room temperature
1 large egg
1 cup smooth peanut butter
1 teaspoon vanilla
½ teaspoon salt
½ teaspoon baking soda
1 ½ cups flour

Equipment

Baking sheet
Baking bowl
Fork
Mixing bowl
Hand mix

 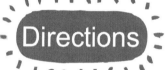

Directions

1. Allow the oven to heat for a while at 180°C.
2. Grease a baking sheet.
3. In a large bowl, cream together sugar and butter.
4. Beat egg into mixture.
5. Mix in peanut butter and vanilla until smooth and creamy.
6. Stir in salt, baking soda and flour until well combined.
7. Roll dough into 1 inch ball and then roll in sugar.
8. Use a long pronged fork to flatten cookies slightly, then turn fork to flatten slightly again. This should create smaller rectangular shape.
9. Bake cookies in the heated oven, one sheet at a time, for about 15 minutes. The color of the cookies will change and it will look slightly under-baked
10. Place it on a baking sheet for 5 minutes to get cool, then transfer to a wire rack to cool completely.
11. You can now enjoy your cookies!

ROCKY ROAD COOKIE CUPS

Serving: 24 people
Baking Time: 12 minutes
Plus Cooling Time: 45 minutes

Ingredients

1 tube (16-½ ounces) refrigerated chocolate chip cookie dough
¾ cup miniature marshmallows
2 tablespoons miniature semisweet chocolate chips
¼ cup sliced almonds, toasted

Equipment

Frying pan
Measuring spoon

Directions

1. Allow the oven to heat for a while at 180°C.
2. Shape dough into 1¼ inches balls.
3. Pick 24 muffin cups and press your dough into its bottom and up sides.
4. Bake until edges are golden, 12 minutes.
5. Roll each piece of cookie dough into prepared muffin cups and press down with your thumb to make a well in the center, or use the back of a measuring teaspoon to make an indentation in each cup.
6. Allow it to bake for 12 minutes or until edges have set and the centers are slightly soft. While still warm, top each cookie cup with ¼ teaspoon of chocolate chips, sprinkle with almonds and 3 marshmallows.
7. Place the cookie cups back in the oven for 2 minutes and allow it to heat again
8. Observe while the marshmallows enlarge and turn brown.
9. Remove from the oven and it let it coo

PIXIE DUST COOKIES

Serving: 42 people
Baking Time: 10 minutes
Plus Cooling Time: 45 minutes

Ingredients

¾ cup plus 2 tablespoons butter, softened
¼ cup sugar
2 cups all-purpose flour
Pearl dust

Equipment

Measuring spoon
Cookie scoop
Mixing bowl
Hand mixer

Directions

1. Allow the oven to heat for a while at 180°C.
2. In a large bowl, cream butter and sugar. Also, beat in flour (dough will be crumbly). Shape rounded spoonfuls of dough into balls, or use a cookie scoop to get the perfect shape.
3. On a lightly floured surface, press dough to ½ inch thickness. Then slightly curve out pixie-shaped cookie cutter in an ungreased baking sheet.
4. Sprinkle with pearl dust.
5. Beat in egg and gradually blend in the dry ingredients.
6. Roll each ball in and place on a greased or lined cookie sheet, about 2 inches apart.
7. Top each ball with a pinch of glitter stars.
8. Bake for 10 minutes in the heated oven. The cookies should appear puffy when first removed but will take shape as they cool.
9. Allow to settle on the rack for 2 minute

GIANT SHARING COOKIES

Serving: 20 people
Baking Time: 18 minutes
Plus Cooling Time: 30 minutes

Ingredients

125 gram Butter (Unsalted)
115 gram Billington's Light Muscovado Sugar
110 gram Billington's Golden Caster Sugar
1 Egg (Large)
220 gram Self Rising Flour
1 teaspoon Salt
2 tablespoon Cocoa Powder

Equipment

Aluminum Foil
Card Board
Scissors
Round Flan Tin
Cake tin
Whisk

Directions

1. Allow the oven to heat for a while at 180°C.
2. Grease and line the base of a 25cm round cake tin.
3. Divide the cake tin into 6 rectangular sizes using strips of card and use the foil to wrap each rectangular.
4. Fold the foil in half and place the points in the middle of the cake tin to divide the tin into 6 segments.
5. Apply cream to both the butter and sugars and add the egg and vanilla.
6. Mix in the flour and salt to soften the dough.
7. Make sure that the mixture is divided into two equal amounts (about 315g).
8. Apply cocoa powder to one of the divided half and mix to make chocolate dough.
9. Further divide each dough to 3 equal parts (approximately 105 gram each)
10. Place dough into one chocolate piece and mix the chocolate chips.
11. Press this into one of the foil segments. The cookie pizza looks best if you alternate vanilla and chocolate segments
12. Let it bake in the heated oven for 18 minutes.
13. Allow it to cool in the tin. The cookie will be hard when it is cool.

PEANUT BUTTER KISS COOKIES

Serving: 36 people
Baking Time: 10 minutes
Plus Cooling Time: 45 minutes

Ingredients

2 cup granulated sugar
½ cup packed brown sugar
½ cup creamy peanut butter
½ cup butter, softened
1 egg
½ cup all-purpose flour (Gold Medal™)
¾ teaspoon baking soda
½ teaspoon baking powder
Additional granulated sugar

Equipment

Measuring bowl
Electric mixer
Measuring spoon

Directions

1. Allow the oven to heat for a while at 180°C.
2. In a large bowl, beat 1½ cup granulated sugar, brown sugar, peanut butter, butter and egg with electric mixer on moderate speed because of the presence of the egg or mix with spoon until well blended.
3. Stir in flour, baking soda and baking powder. Be patient with it as it forms the dough.
4. Shape each dough into 1 inch ball
5. Add in more granulated sugar. On the ungreased cookie sheets, the distance between each dough should not be more than 2 inches apart.
6. Bake for about 10 minutes or until edges are light golden brown.
7. Immediately the cookie is removed from the oven, apply one milk chocolate candy in center of each cookie.
8. Remove the cookies from cookie sheets to cooling rack.

EARTH COOKIES

Serving: 18 people
Baking Time: 9 minutes
Plus Cooling Time: 45 minutes

Ingredients

1 cup butter
1 cup granulated sugar
1½ teaspoons Vanilla
1 Egg
3 cups all purpose Flour
2 teaspoons baking Powder
¼ teaspoon wilton gel colours in Royal Blue
¼ teaspoon of Wilton Gel Colours in Kelly Green

Equipment

Parchment sheet
Measuring spoon
Hand mixer
Mixing bowl
Stand mix

Directions

1. Allow the oven to heat for a while at 180°C.
2. Prepare two baking sheets with parchment paper.
3. Prepare sugar cookie mix according to package Directions.
4. Put about ¼ of dough in one bowl and dye green using green food coloring until desired color is reached. Dye remaining dough blue until desired color is reached.
5. Bring together different pieces from each color and start shaping into a 1" ball, patching if necessary to mould an Earth effect.
6. Put cookie dough in a prepared baking baking sheet and bake for 9 minutes. Be observant and watchful as the dough changes color. Make sure it does not turn brown. Then remove from the oven and allow it to cool for like 2 minute.

MILK 'N' COOKIES ICEBOX CAKE

Serving: 7 people

Baking Time:

Plus Cooling Time: 6 hours 20 minutes

Ingredients

2 boxes Chips Ahoy

3 cups heavy cream

Block cream cheese, softened

2 tablespoon powdered sugar

Equipment

Measuring cup

Refrigerator

Handheld electric mixer

Cake plate

Directions

1. In a large resealable bag, break 15 Chips Ahoy into pieces until 1 cup is crushed.
2. Apply the crushed cookies to a large bowl and pour 3 cups heavy cream and let it ferment for 10 minutes.
3. Then separate heavy cream over mesh strainer; discard the crushed cookies.
4. Use a large mixing bowl with a handheld electric mixer, beat cream cheese until it is soft in 1 minute, then add sugar and beat until it is smooth.
5. Add cookie that has heavy cream and beat until medium peaks form.
6. Apply whipped cream on the surface of a cake plate.
7. Put series of circled cookies on the plate and three in the center.
8. Spread a layer of whipped cream on top and top with another layer of cookies.
9. Change their positions and make sure the cookies are not placed immediately on top of the previous one. Repeat until you have six layers, ending with whipped cream.
10. Top with crushed cookies and wrap loosely with plastic wrap.
11. Transfer to the fridge until very soft. This should take 6 hours.

LEAF COOKIES

Serving: 48 people

Baking Time: 7 minutes

Plus Cooling Time: 1 hour 35 minutes

Ingredients

½ cup butter or margarine, softened

½ cup shortening

1 cup sugar

1½ teaspoons vanilla

2 eggs

3 cups all-purpose flour

½ teaspoon baking soda

½ teaspoon salt

Yellow food color

Red food color

Green food color

Equipment

Hand mixer

Mixing bowl

Cookie sheet

Wire rack

Measuring spoon

Measuring cup

Leaf shaped cookie cutter

Cloth covered surface

Cookie sheet

Directions

1. Allow the oven to heat for a while at 195°C.
2. Stir together sugar, butter and shortening in a large bowl.
3. Stir in vanilla and the 2 eggs.
4. Mix together baking soda, flour and salt.
5. Divide dough into 3 equal parts.
6. Mix 8 drops of orange food color into 1 part of dough to make orange dough. Follow the same process to make yellow and brown dough.
7. In a lightly floured cloth-covered surface, add randomly smaller portions of each of the 3 colors of dough close together.
8. Mould and roll all the dough together into a marbled pattern to 1/8 inch thickness.
9. Cut with 3-inch leaf-shaped cookie cutter and place them about 2 inches apart on ungreased cookie sheet.
10. Allow it to bake for 7 minutes and watch while it bakes.
11. Remove from cookie sheet to wire rack.
12. Cool completely, about 30 minutes.

BANANA ANGEL DELIGHT COOKIES

Serving: 8 people
Baking Time: 15 minutes
Plus Cooling Time: 45 minutes

Ingredients

150 gram caster sugar
1 large egg
200 gram plain flour
Soften butter
1 teaspoon baking powder
1 sachet of banana Angel Delight
70 gram fudge (chopped into pieces)

Equipment

Baking tray
Greaseproof paper
Scissors
Mixing bowl
Wooden spoon

 Directions

1. Allow the oven to heat for a while at 195°C.
2. Neatly cut with sheets of greaseproof paper and put it in line with the baking tray with a pair of kitchen scissors.
3. Stir sugar and soften butter in a mixing bowl by using wooden spoon.
4. Add egg and mix together.
5. Carefully add flour and baking powder to the rest of the ingredients in the bowl.
6. Allow the flour to mix properly with other ingredients.
7. Stir in the bowl packet of banana Angel Delight and chopped fudge in smaller pieces.
8. Use spoon to shape into cookies. Make sure the cookies are 2 inches apart on a tray that is covered in sweet smelling mixture.
9. Allow it to bake for 15 minutes then transfer it to wire rack as it cools.

PENCIL SUGAR COOKIES

Serving: 24 people
Baking Time: 15 minutes
Plus Cooling Time: 20 minutes

Ingredients

24 sugar wafer cookies
1½ cup white chocolate chips
1 tablespoon coconut oil
Pink food coloring
Mini chocolate chips

Equipment

Parchment paper
Baking sheet
Knife
Microwave safe bowl
Mixing bowl

Directions

1. Bring together a large baking sheet with parchment paper.
2. Cut each wafer cookie to create a point on the two diagonal end by using knife.
3. Use a microwave safe bowl to heat white chocolate chips at some percentage of electrical power in 30 second intervals.
4. Monitor the chocolate chips until it melts. Then add in coconut oil and separate into two bowls.
5. In a bowl of melted white chocolate, add in a couple drops of pink food coloring.
6. Dip the flat end of each cookie into a bowl of pink chocolate to create the eraser.
7. Dip the pointed end of each cookie into a bowl of white chocolate to make the tip. Put a mini chocolate chip at the sharp end of each pencil like cookie.
8. Allow it to sit for 15 minutes, and then your pencil sugar cookie is ready!

MONSTER COOKIES

Serving: 24 people
Baking Time: 15 minutes
Plus Cooling Time: 20 minutes

Ingredients

1 cup sugar
1 cup packed light brown sugar
½ cup (1 stick) unsalted butter
3 large eggs
1½ cups peanut butter (smooth)
1 tablespoon vanilla extract
2 teaspoons baking soda
½ teaspoon salt
4½ cups oats (Old Fashioned)
1 cup mini M&Ms
1 cup mini-chocolate chips
Candy eyes

Equipment

Baking sheet
Parchment paper
Mixing bowl
Hand mixer
Measuring spoon

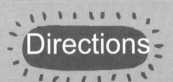 Directions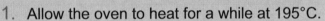

1. Allow the oven to heat for a while at 195°C.
2. Line a large baking sheet with parchment paper
3. In a mixing bowl, cream together the sugar, brown sugar and butter. Mix until it is light and soft.
4. Stir in the eggs and then beat in the peanut butter, vanilla, baking soda and salt until they are evenly combined.
5. Add in the oats (quick) and mix until combined, then add the mini M&Ms and mini-chocolate chips.
6. Take 3 tablespoon mounds of the dough onto the prepared baking sheets, spacing the mounds at least 2 inches apart.
7. Allow the cookies to bake for 15 minutes then remove them from the oven
8. Allow to cool for 5 minutes on the baking sheets.
9. Transfer the cookies to a rack to cool completely.

CHOCOLATE AND PEANUT BUTTER CRISPY BARS

Serving: 16 people
Baking Time: 10 minutes
Plus Cooling Time: 2 hours 10 minutes

Ingredients

3 cups brown rice crisps
1¼ cups whole pecans, chopped, divided
¾ cup creamy peanut butter (plus a pinch of salt if your peanut butter is unsalted)
½ cup honey
1½ cups (9 ounces)
Chocolate chips
¼ teaspoon kitchen salt

Equipment

Parchment paper
Baking dish
Hand mixer
Measuring spoon
Saucepan
Mixing bowl
Silicone spatula

Directions

1. Put parchment paper of about 8 inches in a baking dish
2. Cut to fit neatly across the base and up opposite sides.
3. Stir in a bowl, brown rice crisps and 1 cup of the chopped pecans.
4. Add in a saucepan peanut butter and honey.
5. Allow the mixture to steam in a low mixer heat as you watch the mixture bring bubbles. Then apply rice crispy to the bowl.
6. Use a silicone spatula to stir until the mixture has blended
7. Then put every ingredient in the lined baking dish.
8. Apply gentle force on the spatula to spread it fairly evenly.
9. Switch to a large, sturdy glass with a flat bottom (mason jar) and press down firmly allover, including the corners. Then use your hand to mix the ingredients evenly.
10. Melt the chocolate chips in a microwave-safe bowl in every 30-second, stirring after each one.
The chocolate is done when it's about 90 percent melted. Continue stirring even after it is off the heat.
11. Add the melted chocolate on the peanut butter-crispy mixture. Use spatula to spread it evenly all over then sprinkle the remaining pecans and salt on the top.
12. Put the baking dish in the refrigerator for 2 hours.
13. To slice, carefully grab both sides of the parchment paper and lift it out of the baking dish.
14. Use knife to make 4 even columns and 4 even rows.
15. Avoid risk of cracking the chocolate. Carefully apply even pressure from above the knife to press straight down, rather than sawing from one edge across.

PORRIDGE BARS

Serving: 8 people
Baking Time: 1 hour
Plus Cooling Time: 1 hour 45 minutes

Ingredients

130gram rolled oats
5 dried apricots
25gram dried cranberries
30gram raisins
15gram sunflower seeds
10gram seeds
1 teaspoon cinnamon
300milimetre milk
1 large egg
1 teaspoon vanilla extract

Equipment

Mixing bowl
Scissors
Fork
Measuring jug

Directions

1. Allow the oven to heat for a while at 180°C.
2. Add the rolled oats into a mixing bowl.
3. Add snipped apricots, dried cranberries and raisins into the bowl.
4. Once all of the dried fruits have been added, move your attention to the nuts and seeds. If you are using nuts, you may need to chop them into smaller pieces before adding to the bowl.
5. Sprinkle pumpkin seed and sunflower on it. Then the ground cinnamon.
6. Pour milk and eggs into a measuring jug and stir with a fork then add vanilla extract.
7. Pour the ingredients into the mixing bowl with ingredients then mix together.
8. Let the oats take control of the milk and egg soaking them up, while you dig out your square baking tin and line the base and sides with greaseproof or parchment paper.
9. Put the mixture in the prepared parchment paper then observe the oats floating in a sea of milk.
10. Bake it for 1 hour
11. Allow it to cool in the tin.

MALTESERS COOKIES

Serving: 36 people
Baking Time: 10 minutes
Plus Cooling Time: 25 minutes

Ingredients

1 cup unsalted butter
½ cup white sugar
1 cup brown sugar
2 eggs
1 teaspoon vanilla extract
2¼ cups all purpose flour
1 teaspoon baking soda
1 teaspoon sea salt
2 cups roughly chopped malted milk balls (Maltesers)

Equipment

Baking sheet
Parchment paper
Mixing bowl
Measuring spoon
Hand mixer
Wooden spoon

Directions

1. Allow the oven to heat for a while at 180°C then line baking sheets with parchment paper.
2. Mix butter smooth in a large bowl using a hand mixer and add sugar.
3. Allow it to be soft and light, and then add eggs and vanilla.
4. Mix and ensure everything is evenly mixed.
5. Add the flour, salt, and baking soda to a separate bowl and stir them together.
6. Then mix the two bowls of ingredients together by adding the flour mixture into the butter mixture.
7. Stir slowly to ensure all are neatly mixed but avoid spillage.
8. Add in the chopped Maltesers and stir them in with a wooden spoon.
9. Mould each dough into balls about 1½ tablespoons at a time and place the balls on the cookie sheets, about 12 to a large sheet (8 to a small sheet).
10. Bake for about 10 minutes, or until the edges of the cookies become slightly brown.
11. It's a good idea to watch them after about 8 minutes of baking.
12. Let the cookies cool on the pan for several minutes.

ROLO COOKIE CUPS

Serving: 16 people
Baking Time: 15 minutes
Plus Cooling Time: 20 minutes

Ingredients

115g unsalted butter, softened
115g light soft brown sugar
1 large egg
225g plain flour
½ teaspoon bicarbonate of soda

Equipment

Mini muffin tin
Mixing bowl
Electric mixer
Wooden spoon

Directions

1. Allow the oven to heat for a while at 170°C.
2. Add the softened butter and sugar into a mixing bowl.
3. Mix and use electric mixer to mix together until they are light and soft.
4. Add egg, the flour and bicarbonate of soda.
5. Use a wooden spoon to stir everything together.
6. Take a handful of dough in a ball size and place them into each hole in your tin. Flour can be added to hands so as not to get sticky.
7. Immediately the cookie cups are out of the oven, put a Rolo into the middle of each one. The cookie cups will be very hot so be careful!
8. Leave the Rolo cookie cups to stick as it cools in the tin.

SAND DOLLAR COOKIES

Serving: 18 people
Baking Time: 15 minutes
Plus Cooling Time: 1 hour 45 minutes

Ingredients

1½ cups butter, softened
2/3 cup confectioners' sugar
3 tablespoons sugar
4 teaspoons almond extract
2 2/3 cups all-purpose flour
½ teaspoon salt
2 large eggs, lightly beaten
Slivered almonds and cinnamon sugar

Equipment

Mixing bowl
Hand mixer
Plastic
Refrigerator
Round cookie cutter
Spatula
Baking sheet
Wire rack

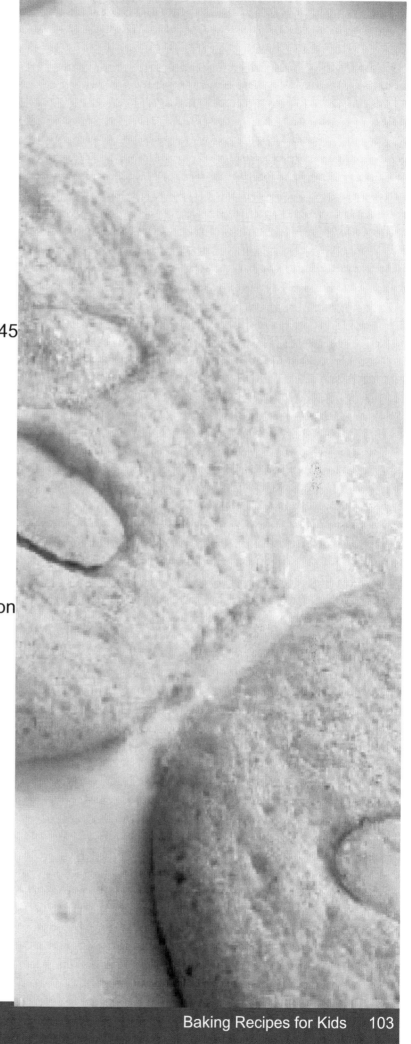

Directions

1. Beat butter and sugar in a large mixing bowl until it gets light and soft.
2. Gradually add the flour and salt and mix well.
3. Divide dough in half. Use your hand or a tool to shape each dough into a disk and wrap in plastic.
4. Put it in a refrigerator for 1 hour.
5. Allow the oven to heat for a while at 185°C, and then roll each portion of dough between waxed paper to 1/8 inch thickness.
6. Use a 3 inches round cookie cutter dipped in flour to cut. Using a floured spatula, place 1 inch apart on ungreased baking sheets.
7. Try to brush with egg and decorate with almonds to resemble sand dollars and sprinkle with cinnamon sugar.
8. Allow it to bake for 16 minutes
9. Allow it to cool for 2 minutes before removing to wire racks.

TEDDY BEAR COOKIES

Serving: 18 people
Baking Time: 8 minutes
Plus Cooling Time: 1 hour 55 minutes

Ingredients

1 cup sugar
¾ cup Butter, softened (Land O Lakes®)
1 large Egg (Land O Lakes®)
2 teaspoons vanilla
2 ¼ cups all-purpose flour
1 teaspoon baking powder
¼ teaspoon salt
2 (1-ounce) squares unsweetened baking chocolate, melted

Equipment

Mixing bowl
Cookie sheet
Fork
Measuring spoon
Measuring cup
Hand mixer

Directions

1. Allow the oven to heat for a while at 185°C.
2. Beat sugar, butter, egg and vanilla in a mixing bowl. Allow it to mix properly.
3. Then add flour, baking powder and salt. Stir gently at low speed, scraping the bowl often, until it is evenly mixed.
4. Divide the dough into 2 halves.
5. Place half a dough into another bowl.
6. Stir in chocolate until well mixed.
7. Now try to shape each teddy bear using either vanilla or chocolate dough or a combination of two-toned teddy bears.
8. Shape one large 1-inch ball for body.
9. Place onto ungreased cookie sheet; flatten slightly.
10. Shape one medium ¾-inch ball for head, 4 small ½-inch balls for the arms and legs, then 2 smaller balls for ears.
11. Put head, arms, legs and ears by overlapping slightly onto body. Attach small balls for eyes, noseand mouth. Use fork to make claws on paws.
12. Leave it to bake for 8 minutes then allow it to cool for 1 minute on cookie sheet.

MARSHMALLOW FLOWER COOKIES

Serving: 26 people

Baking Time: 10 minutes

Plus Cooling Time: 40 minutes

Ingredients

2 dozen cooked & cooled sugar cookies

2 tablespoon milk

½ teaspoon vanilla extract

1½ cups powdered sugar

Jelly beans (24 green ones & 24 yellow ones)

12 cup Peanut Butter (Mini Reese)

Mini marshmallows

Colored sugar sprinkles yellow & pink

Equipment

Measuring spoon

Measuring cup

Mixing bowl

Hand mixer

 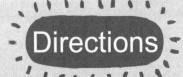

1. Allow the oven to heat for a while at 185°C.
2. Beat together the softened butter and powdered sugar into a mixing bowl and add milk to stir consistency until the desired result is gotten.
3. Mix in the vanilla extract and 2 drops of blue food coloring to give it a beautiful color.
4. Stylishly cut mini Reese's cups in half and place each half towards the bottom of each cookie.
5. Arrange 1 green jelly bean lengthwise above the peanut butter cup.
6. Cut each mini marshmallow diagonally, and then dip the sticky part into the colored sugar.
7. Arrange the marshmallow halves around the top of the cookie in a circular shape, leaving enough room for the yellow jelly bean in the middle.
8. Repeat the process for each cookie until you have an entire garden in your kitchen!

ANIMAL COOKIES

Serving: 60 people
Baking Time: 10 minutes
Plus Cooling Time: 1 hour 38 minutes

Ingredients

12 tablespoons butter, softened (170gram)
¼ cup sugar (50gram)
3 tablespoons honey (64gram)
½ teaspoon salt
½ teaspoon baking soda
1 teaspoon vanilla extract
1½ cups All-Purpose Flour (177gram)
1 cup oat flour (99gram)

Equipment

Mixing bowl
Hand mixer
Measuring spoon
Measuring cup
Baking sheet
Parchment paper
Animal cookie cutter

Directions

1. Beat together the butter and sugar.
2. Allow it to mix properly then add honey, salt, baking soda, and flavor and stir gently until they are well mixed.
3. Add the flour and oat flour and mix. This time the solution needs patience so gently but consistently stir as they are evenly mixed.
4. Equally divide the dough into 2 halves
5. Beat each half until slightly flat so that it is able to make a disk, and then wrap in plastic. When that is done, put it in the refrigerator for 1 hour to ferment.
6. Remove one piece of dough out of the refrigerator, and turn it out onto a lightly floured surface. Roll the dough ¼ thick and 2-inches apart for the next cookie.
7. Allow the oven to heat for a while at 185°C. Then lightly grease several baking sheets, or line them with parchment and place the animal cookies on them.
8. Cut with the animal cookie cutter into the parchment paper.
9. Bake the cookies for 10 minutes, until you can see yourself that the color is changing.
10. Remove it from the oven and allow it to cool on the baking sheet for some minutes.
11. Then transfer it to wire rack to cool completely.

PLANET COOKIES

Serving: 30 people

Baking Time: 15 minutes

Plus Cooling Time: 24 minutes

Ingredients

400gram plain flour

500gram dark Muscovado sugar

2 eggs

180gram cocoa powder

2½ teaspoons baking powder

¼ teaspoon salt

370gram softened butter

You will also need round cookie cutters in various sizes.

Chocolate Planet Cookies in various colors

Equipment

Mixing bowl

Hand mixer

Electric mixer

Measuring spoon

Measuring cup

Baking tray

Baking paper

Round cookie cutter of various sizes

Directions

1. Beat the butter and sugar together in a large mixing bowl until it's light and soft.
2. Mix the eggs in the bowl.
3. Add the dry ingredients in the mixing bowl and mix together until the mixture starts to form a dough.
4. Use your hand to continue to mix until it becomes easy to knead.
5. Use your hand to shape the dough into one or two large balls and wrap with cling-film. Then, put it in the refrigerator for one to two hours. This makes the dough easier to roll out and cut.
6. Allow the oven to heat for a while at 170°C.
7. Once the dough has chilled, roll out, using extra flour to make sure that it does not stick. The dough should be rolled out to around 8 millimetres thick. Cut out circle shapes in various sizes using cookie cutters.
8. After cutting the cookies into sizes put it in the tray and bake in the oven for 15 minutes.
9. Allow to cool completely.

CHAPTER SIX

Hungry Caterpillar Cupcakes

Serving: 24 People

Baking Time: 15 to 20 minutes

Plus Cooling Time: 1 hour

Cupcake ingredients:

180g butter

1/2 cup of sugar

1 teaspoon of vanilla flavor

3 eggs

2 1/2 cup of flour

3 teaspoon baking powder

1/2 cup of milk

Icing ingredients:

250g of butter

6 cups of icing sugar

1 teaspoon of vanilla extract

1/2 cup of milk

Green and red food coloring

Equipment

Oven

Directions

1. Heat the oven to 180°C.
2. Line the cupcake tray with the paper cases.
3. Cream the butter, sugar and vanilla flavor in a bowl.
4. Add the beaten eggs, flour, baking powder and milk.
5. Spoon mixture into the tray. Bake for 15 to 20 minutes and cool for 30 minutes.

For the icing:

1. Cream the butter, icing sugar, vanilla extract and milk.
2. Divide icing in two and color one green.
3. Arrange the cupcakes in the curvy shape of a caterpillar.
4. Pipe the green icing on all the cakes except the one that'll be used as the head.
5. Color the remaining icing red and use it to ice the head cake.
6. Use the leftover green icing to decorate it and give it eyes.

LEMON EXTRACT CUPCAKES

Serving: 12 cupcakes
Baking Time: 15 to 20 minutes
Plus Cooling Time: 35 to 50 minutes

Cake ingredients:

115g of butter
115g of flour
115g of sugar
5ml of lemon extract
2 eggs

Icing ingredients:

110g of butter
175g of icing sugar
5ml of lemon extract
Yellow food coloring

Equipment

Oven
Cupcakes tray
Cupcake paper cases
Piping bag and nozzle
Bowls and spatula for mixing

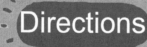

Directions

1. Heat the oven to 180°C.
2. Line the cupcake tray with the paper cases.
3. Beat the butter and sugar together until it is creamy.
4. Beat the eggs and pour it in gradually.
5. Add the flour and mix together until it is well mixed.
6. Pour the batter into the cupcake tray and bake for 15 - 20 minutes.
7. Remove from oven and allow to cool for 10 minutes before removing it from the pan.
8. Put it on a rack for about 15 minutes for it to completely cool.
9. For the icing, beat the butter and icing sugar together.
10. Add the extract and food coloring. Color to your taste.
11. Put the icing in a piping bag and apply to the cold cupcakes.
12. Your cupcakes are ready to eat!

GREEN VELVET CUPCAKES

Serving: 18 cupcakes
Baking Time: 15 to 20 minutes
Plus Cooling Time: 35 to 50 minutes

Cupcake ingredients:

225g of butter
225g of sugar
195g of flour
1/2 teaspoon of baking powder
1/4 teaspoon of salt
3 eggs
1 teaspoon vanilla extract
30g cocoa powder
Green food coloring

Icing ingredients:

100g of cheese cream
100g of butter
400g of icing sugar
1 teaspoon lemon juice
Green sprinkle decorations

Equipment

Oven
Piping bag and nozzle
Bowls and spatula
Cupcake pans and paper cases
Cooling rack

Directions

1. Heat the oven to 180°C.
2. Line the cupcake tray with the paper cases.
3. Cream the butter and sugar in a bowl.
4. Add coloring, eggs, vanilla extract, salt, baking powder and mix properly.
5. Add flour and cocoa powder to the mixture.
6. Mix well and spoon into the tray.
7. Allow to bake for about 15 to 20 minutes and remove from oven.
8. Cool for 10 minutes before removing from the pan to the cooling rack.
9. Beat the cream cheese and butter together.
10. Add the lemon juice and icing sugar and mix together until it's very smooth.
11. Use the piping bag to apply the icing to the cupcake.

Butterfly Cakes

Serving: 10 cupcakes
Baking time: 15 to 20 minutes
Plus Cooling Time: 35 to 50 minutes

Cupcake ingredients:

110g of butter
110g of sugar
2 eggs
1 teaspoon of vanilla extract
110g of flour
1/4 teaspoon of salt
1/2 teaspoon of baking powder
3 tablespoon of milk

Ingredients for icing:

300g of icing sugar
150g of butter
2 teaspoon of vanilla extract

Equipment:

Oven
Piping bag and nozzle
Bowls and spatula
Cupcake pans
Cupcake paper cases
Cooling rack

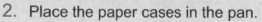

Directions

1. Heat the oven to 180°C.
2. Place the paper cases in the pan.
3. Cream the butter and sugar in a bowl.
4. Stir in the eggs, vanilla extract, salt, baking powder, milk and flour.
5. Scoop batter into the tray.
6. Bake for about 20 minutes.
7. Allow to cool for 10 minutes in the pan.
8. Put the cake in the rack to cool completely.
9. Beat the butter, icing sugar and vanilla extract.
10. Neatly cut off the tops of the cooled cupcakes and slice it in half.
11. Spread your icing on the other half of the cake.
12. Gently push the sliced tops to spread and form the shape of a butterfly's wings with it.
13. There you go with your butterfly cakes!

BISCOFF CUPCAKES

Serving: 12 cupcakes
Baking Time: 20 to 25 minutes
Plus Cooling Time: 35 to 55 minutes

Cupcake ingredients:

150g of butter
150g of sugar
3 eggs
150g self-rising flour
1/2 teaspoon baking powder
1/2 teaspoon vanilla extract

Icing ingredients:

175g of butter
350g of icing sugar
2 tablespoons of milk
200g of lotus biscuit spread
10 lotus biscuits

Equipment

Oven
Piping bag and nozzle
Bowls and spatula
Cupcake pans and paper cases
Cooling rack

Directions

1. Heat the oven to 180°C.
2. Place the paper cases into the cupcake tray.
3. Cream the butter and sugar in a bowl.
4. Stir in the eggs, vanilla extract, baking powder and flour.
5. Spoon the batter into the tray.
6. Bake for 20 to 25 minutes.
7. Allow to cool for 10 minutes before removing cupcakes from the tray to the rack to cool completely.

For the Frosting:

1. Beat the butter, icing sugar, biscuit spread and milk together.
2. Mix till it's fluffy and put in piping bag.
3. Carve out the centre of the cooled cake with a sharp knife.
4. Put in the icing.
5. Cover with the carved out cake and ice it all together.
6. Add a lotus biscuit on top for style.

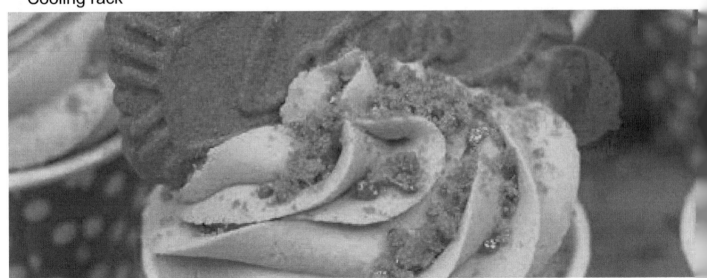

GARDEN BIRTHDAY CAKE

Serving: 12 people
Baking Time: 30 to 40 minutes
Plus Cooling Time: 1 hour

Cupcake ingredients:

250g of self-rising flour
1 teaspoon baking powder
1 teaspoon mixed spice
225g of sugar
4 eggs
200ml sunflower oil
1 orange zest
125g of grated carrots
125g of grated beetroot

Ingredients for the icing:

100g of butter
200g of cheese cream
1 teaspoon of vanilla extract
100g of sugar
40g raw beetroot (optional)
Edible flower decorations

Equipment

Oven
Piping bag and nozzle
Bowls and spatula
Cupcake pan and paper cases
Cooling rack

Directions

1. Heat the oven to 180°C.
2. Line the cupcake tray with the paper cases.
3. Mix the flour, baking powder, sugar and mixed spice together.
4. Whisk the eggs, sunflower oil and orange zest in another bowl and add to the flour mixture.
5. Divide mixture in two.
6. Pour beetroot gratings in one and carrots in the other and pour into different tins.
7. Bake for 30 to 40 minutes.
8. Allow to cool for 10 minutes before removing cupcakes from the tin to cool completely.
9. Beat the butter, vanilla extract and sugar together. Stir in cream cheese and/or beetroot.
10. Ice the cakes and decorate with different edible flower decorations.

CONFETTI CAKE BATTER COOKIES

Serving: 34 people
Baking Time: 6 to 8 minutes
Plus Cooling Time: 16 to 18 minutes

Cupcake ingredients:

1 box of cake mix
1 teaspoon of baking powder
1/3 cup of oil
2 eggs
1/2 teaspoon vanilla extract
1 cup of sprinkles

Equipment:

Bowls and spatula
Cookie sheet
Parchment paper
Oven
Cooling rack

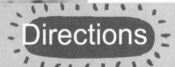

Directions

1. Heat the oven to 180°C.
2. Line a cookie sheet with parchment paper and set aside.
3. Stir the cake mix and baking powder in a bowl.
4. Whisk eggs, oil and vanilla extract in another bowl and add to flour mixture.
5. Stir very well.
6. Pour in the cup of sprinkles.
7. Mix it very well and make sure it spreads evenly.
8. Take a tablespoon of dough and shape it into 1-inch balls.
9. Place them on cookie sheets. Let them be one inch apart.
10. Take a glass, dip the bottom into flour and use it to flatten out the dough to about 1/4 inch.
11. Bake for 6 to 8 minutes.
12. Let it cool for 1 minute before removing from cookie sheet to cooling rack.
13. After 10 minutes, spread your icing over warm cookies and sprinkle with candy sprinkles.
14. Store in an airtight container.

CUTE CHICK CAKE POPS

Serving: 25 People
Baking Time: 20 to 25 minutes
Plus Cooling Time: 35 to 50 minutes

Cake ingredients:

120g of flour
140g of sugar
1/2 teaspoon of baking powder
40g of butter
120ml of milk
1 egg

Icing ingredients:

125g of butter
1 teaspoon of vanilla extract
300g icing sugar
2 teaspoon of milk

Decorations:

100g of yellow chocolate buttons
Yellow food coloring
Orange food coloring

Equipment

Paper lollipop sticks
8 inches round cake pan
Fridge
Bowls
Spatula

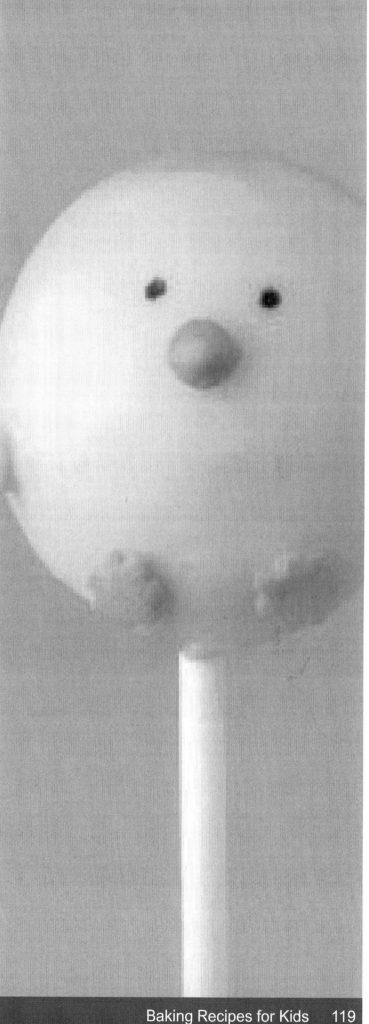

Directions

1. Heat the oven to 150°C and grease the cake pan.
2. Cream butter and sugar.
3. Add flour, baking powder, beaten eggs and milk.
4. Mix together and pour into cake pan.
5. Bake for 20 to 25 minutes.
6. Allow to cool for 5 minutes before removing from pan.
7. Break it into pieces for it to cool completely.

For The Frosting

1.
2. Cream the butter and icing sugar.
3. Add the vanilla extract and milk. Set aside.
4. Break the completely cooled cake into fine pieces in a bowl.
5. Pour the cake pieces into the frosting; just enough to mould the cake pieces.
6. Mould the pieces into balls and put in the fridge for 30 minutes to solidify.
7. Melt the chocolate buttons completely.
8. Dip a stick into the chocolate and push half of it into the molded cake.
9. Using the sticks, completely dip the balls into the remaining chocolate and decorate it.
10. Your Cute Chick Cake Pops is ready!

GERMAN CHOCOLATE DUMP CAKE

Serving: 16 people
Baking Time: 35 to 40 minutes
Plus Cooling Time: 45 to 60 minutes

Ingredients

1 cup of sweetened flaked coconut
1/2 cup of chopped pecans
1 box of cake mix
1/2 cup of butter
200g of creamed cheese
1 teaspoon of vanilla extract
1/4 teaspoon salt
2 cups of sugar
1/2 cup of semi-sweet chocolate chips

Equipment

Round cake pan
Bowls and spatula
Cooling rack

Directions

1. Heat the oven to 350 degrees and grease the cake pan.
2. Prepare the cake mix accordingly.
3. Sprinkle the coconut flakes and one cup of chopped pecans at the bottom of the cake pan.
4. Pour the cake mix into the cake pan already containing the coconut flakes and add 1 cup of chopped pecans.
5. Beat the cream cheese, butter, vanilla extract and salt in a bowl.
6. Add the sugar, chocolate chips and the rest of the pecans into the mixture.
7. Scoop the cream cheese mixture into the cake pan.
8. Gently stir the cream cheese mixture with the batter already in the pan using a knife.
9. Bake for 35 to 40 minutes and allow to cool for 10 minutes before removing from pan.

HEARTY SMARTIE CHOCOLATE CAKE

Serving: 12 people
Baking Time: 20 minutes
Plus Cooling Time: 50 minutes

Ingredients

125g of butter
175g sugar
2 eggs
200g self-rising flour
60g cocoa powder
1 teaspoon baking powder
250ml plain yoghurt

For icing:

300g icing sugar
2 tablespoon of cocoa powder
15g of butter

Equipment

Bowls
Spatula
Cooling rack
Cake pans

Directions

1. Heat the oven to 180°C and grease two cake pans.
2. Cream the butter and sugar in a bowl.
3. Whisk the eggs and pour into the mixture.
4. Stir in the flour, baking powder, cocoa powder and plain yoghurt till it's smooth.
5. Pour the mixture into the greased pans and bake for 20 minutes.
6. Let it cool for 10 minutes before removing from the pan to the rack to cool completely.
7. Pour the icing sugar and cocoa powder into a bowl.
8. Melt the butter and add to the icing sugar. Mix it properly.Cover the surface of one cake with half of the icing mixture and place the other cake on it.
9. Spread the remaining icing over the cake and decorate with sweets in the shape of a heart in the Centre and around the edges.

NUMBERS CAKE

Numbers cake or letter cake are awesome, delicious cream and they are decorated flowers for special events like birthday parties and anniversary.

Serving: 8 people
Baking Time: I hour 13 minutes
Plus Cooling Time: 1 hour 25 minutes

Ingredients

300 grams flour
75 grams ground almond
75 grams crumbled sugar
200 grams of cold butter
1 egg
1/2 teaspoon vanilla extract
A little salt

For The Cream:

400 grams of cream cheese
400 milligrams of heavy cream
150 grams of powdered sugar
1 teaspoon of vanilla extract

For Decorations:

Chocolates
Fruits (strawberries)
Flowers

Equipment

Oven
Cupcake tray and paper cases
Piping bag and nozzles
Bowls and spatula for mixing

Directions

1. In a big bowl, mix the butter, flour, crumbled almond, fined sugar and small salt.
2. Stir until specks are formed.
3. Break and add egg with vanilla extract, continue mixing until a dough is formed.
4. Put the dough into a plastic surface and refrigerate for 1 hour.
5. Preheat the oven to 375°F.
6. Cut the alphabet or letter you want, then whirl the dough on a parchment paper and cool for 30 minutes.
7. Bake between 10-13 minutes or wait till it becomes brown in color.
8. Allow it to cool totally.

To Make Cream:

1. In a large bowl, whip the mascarpone and powdered sugar.
2. Whip till it flattens.
3. Afterwards, add your vanilla extract and heavy cream and strike it until it becomes stiff.
4. Transfer the mixture into a piping sachet.
5. Pipe the cream on the cake and make the decoration of your choice.

SORTING HAT CUPCAKES

Serving: 20 people
Baking time: 15 - 25 minutes
Plus Cooling Time: 40minutes

Ingredients

Cupcakes

¾ cup of cocoa powder
¾ cup whole flour
½ teaspoon baking powder
¼ teaspoon of salt
Butter
Sugar
3 big eggs
1 teaspoon of vanilla extract
½ cup of cream
½ cup chocolate chips

Icing ingredients

2 cups of butter
1 teaspoon of vanilla extract
4 cups confectioner's sugar
½ cup of cocoa powder
25 chewy caramels

Equipment

Oven
Cupcake tray and paper cases
Piping bag and nozzles
Bowls and spatula for mixing

Directions

First bake the cupcakes:

1. Mix cocoa powder, flour, baking powder and salt in a bowl and stir thoroughly.
2. In another bowl, whip both butter and sugar with spatula until it is pale and fluffy.
3. Add eggs, vanilla extracts, flour, and cream.
4. Add the chocolate chips and mix until it has blended well.
5. Line a muffin container with parchment paper and divide the batter between the muffin cups.
6. Bake at 350°F for 20-25 minutes.
7. Cool in the pan for 5 minutes, then transfer to a cooling rack and cool.

You can now move to the buttercream: Mix the butter with spatula until pale and fluffy, afterward add vanilla and stir thoroughly. Add the confectioner's sugar and beat for 3-5 minutes, until fluffy.

1. Place the buttercream in a piping bag and decorate the cake.
2. You need to join them together now. Here's how to do that.
3. To prepare the sorting hat:
4. Shape the caramel into a flat disk with your hands.
5. Form another caramel into a cone shape, and glue it to the flat disk.
6. Use knife to build the sorting hat's face.
7. Repeat with the remaining caramels to make a total of 12 sorting hats.
8. Position the sorting hats on top of the baked cake.

VANILLA CUPCAKES

Serving: 14 People
Baking Time: 15 Minutes
Plus Cooling Time: 35 Minutes

Ingredients

165 grams of whole flour
1/4 teaspoon of baking powder
Pinch of salt
115 grams of unsalted butter
200 grams granulated sugar
2 big eggs
2 teaspoon of vanilla extract
120 grams sour cream

Vanilla Frosting:

1 cup (230 grams) unsalted butter, softened
3 cups (360 grams) confectioner's sugar
2 teaspoons vanilla extract
30ml of heavy cream

Equipment

Oven
Cupcake tray and paper cases
Piping bag and nozzles
Bowls and spatula for mixing

Directions

1. Preheat oven to 350°F. Cover the pan with cupcake liners.
2. Using a large bowl, whisk the flour, baking powder, and salt together.
3. Use a hand mixer to paddle and beat the butter and sugar until they become light and fluffy.
4. Crush and add the eggs and the vanilla.
5. Also, add in the sour cream and blend very well.
6. Scoop the batter into the cupcake liners, and bake at 350°F for 18-22 minutes.
7. Take it out from the oven to cool for some time.

To make the frosting

1. Take a bowl and add butter, confectioner's sugar, vanilla and mix slowly until a perfect blend is achieved.
2. Gradually add in the heavy cream, and mix for some time until the frosting is smooth and properly integrated.
3. Frost the cooled cupcakes as desired.

PINK MARBLE SANDWICH CAKE

This is a very delicious cake that can be used as dessert. I am sure you will love it!
Serving: 10 people
Baking Time: 30 Minutes
Plus Cooling Time: 55 Minutes

Ingredients

225 grams of unsalted butter
225 grams of whole flour
6 teaspoons of raspberry jam
225 grams of sugar
4 small eggs
1 teaspoon of milk
250 ml of cream
75 grams of icing

Equipment

Oven
Cupcake tray and paper cases
Piping bag and nozzles
Bowls and spatula

 Directions

1. Preheat oven to 375°F
2. Cover baking pan with parchment paper.
3. In a medium bowl, blend jam with one teaspoon of water, butter and sugar
4. Mix properly with your hand until pale and fluffy
5. Slowly add the broken eggs, and mix carefully
6. Bake inside the oven for 20-25 minutes
7. Cool in tin for 5 minutes before removing from tin
8. Place on a wire rack to cool
9. After cooling, beat the cream and icing sugar. Peel off parchment from cakes and sandwich together with the cream.
10. Your Pink Marble Sandwich Cake is ready to serve!

MILKSHAKE MICE CUPCAKES

Serving: 12
Baking Time: 30 Minutes
Plus Cooling Time: 50 Minutes

Ingredients
For The Cupcakes:

100 grams of unsalted butter
150 grams of whole flour
150 grams of caster sugar
20 grams of strawberry milkshake powder
3 teaspoons of milk
2 big eggs

Icing:

35 grams of unsalted butter
35 grams of caster sugar
80 grams of cream
5 teaspoons of strawberry milkshake powder

Decorations

Mini marshmallows
Chocolate
Jellies
Strawberry sweet

Equipment

Oven
Cupcake tray and paper cases
Piping bag and nozzles
Bowls
Spatula

Directions

1. Preheat the oven to 350°F
2. Mix butter into a mixing bowl, add sugar and mix thoroughly until it is light and fluffy.
3. Add broken eggs into the bowl.
4. Add milk and milkshake powder. Mix thoroughly and place in the pan.
5. Put the mixture inside the oven and allow it to bake for 20 to 25 minutes.

For the icing

1. Mix butter and caster sugar together to become light and fluffy.
2. Stir in the cream cheese and strawberry milkshake powder.
3. Decorate the cupcake with the icing and add the mini marshmallows as the ears, chocolate chips as the eyes, a jelly bean as the nose and a 'shoelace' sweet for the whiskers and tail.
4.

CHAPTER SEVEN

MINI STARS BERRY PIES

Serving: 4 people
Baking Time: 30 minutes
Plus Cooling Time: 120 minutes

Ingredients

1 package of refrigerated rolled pie crusts
Flour
1 large egg (beaten)
1 tablespoon of sugar
1¹/2 cup of fresh berries (blue)
1¹/2 cup of sliced strawberries
1¹/4 cup of new raspberries
1¹/2 tablespoon of cornstarch
A pinch kg kosher salt
Vanilla ice cream

Equipment

Stencil
Collie Cutters
Pie tins

Directions

1. Sprinkle flour on your baking surface.
2. Start with one pie crust. Turn dough on the flour surface making sure that it is ⅛ thick.
3. Use stencil to cut the dough. Keep the scraps.
4. Mold the scraps into half-inch thick.
5. Roll the scraps a little on the surface with flour. Make it ⅛ thick. Then cut out the stars using collie cutters. Reroll the scraps as necessary.
6. Transfer the dough to pie tins.
7. Fold the edge under to align with the edges of the tin.
8. Position pie tins and stars on the baking paper.
9. Brush edges of the dough and stars with beaten egg.
10. Sprinkle both with a tablespoon of sugar. Allow to rest for half an hour.
11. While you wait, heat oven to 350°C.
12. Twirl blueberries, strawberries, raspberries, cornstarch, salt, and remaining quarter cup sugar in a bowl.
13. Allow to sit for ten minutes and toss periodically to make it juicy.
14. Fill pie crust with the fruit mixture.
15. Position stars on pies as desired.
16. Bake the pies until the fruit bubbles. The crust will turn golden brown too. It takes about half an hour for this to happen.
17. Serve desert with ice cream.

MEYER LEMON MERINGUE PIE

Serving: 8 people

Baking Time: 25 minutes

Plus Cooling Time: 4 hours 30 minutes

Ingredients

1 tablespoon of cornstarch

11/4 cup of sugar

2 eggs (plus 4 egg yolks and 3 egg whites)

2 tablespoon of Meyer lemon, add 3/4 cup of lemon juice

6 tablespoons of cold butter (unsalted), cut to pieces

1/8 teaspoon of kosher salt

Half teaspoon of pure vanilla

A jar of marshmallow crème.

Equipment

Dish Pie Plate

Fork

Parchment Paper

Electronic Mixer

Wire Rack

Directions

1. Start by heating the oven to 150°C.
2. Unroll a pie crust and brush it with water.
3. Add the remainder of the pie crust and roll to a circle of 12 inches.
4. Transfer to a deep – dish pie plate. Tuck the ends, and crimp. Stab the bottom with a fork. Then, line pie crust with parchment paper.
5. Fill the pie crust up with dried beans.
6. Bake till the ends are set.
7. Remove the weights as well as the parchment paper.
8. Bake for 9 minutes.
9. Allow to cool completely.
10. Whisk a cup of sugar and cornstarch in a medium sized saucepan together.
11. Add whole eggs, egg yolks, and lemon juice to the saucepan.
12. Set the heat to medium and cook.
13. Whisk the pan regularly till it becomes thick and bubbling. It usually takes 9 minutes.
14. Remove from heat.
15. Stir in lemon zest and butter till everything melts, and becomes smooth.
16. 16.   Beat the egg white and salt on an electric mixer with medium speed.
17. Continue till it becomes foamy.
18. Add the remainder of the quarter cup of sugar slowly.
19. Beat till stiff peaks appear.
20. Add vanilla and beat.
21. Add the marshmallow crème and beat till it all becomes smooth.
22. Spread over the pie.
23. Bake till meringue becomes lightly browned.
24. Allow to cool totally on a wire rack.
25. Refrigerate if you want to.

STRAWBERRY SLAB PIE

Serving: 12 People
Baking Time: 45 minutes
Plus Cooling Time: I hour 15 minutes

Ingredients

3/4 cup of granulated sugar
Pinch salt
Flour for the surface
3 recipes of buttery pie crust
Large egg white
6 tablespoons of cornstarch
1 tablespoon of fresh orange zest
(add 2 tablespoons of fresh orange juice)
1.5 kg strawberries, quartered
11/4 cup of flour
1 teaspoon sugar
Half teaspoon kosher salt
Half cup chill unsalted butter, cut it up
4 tablespoons ice – cold water

Equipment

15 x10 inch pan
Fork
Saucepan

Directions

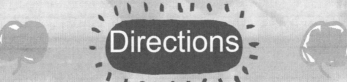

1. Start by making the pie crust. Whisk flour, sugar, and salt together in a bowl.
2. Cut the butter into the mixture till mixture looms like coarse meal.
3. Add water gradually, 1 tablespoon at a time.
4. Use fork to pull dough together into crumbs pile.
5. Add water if necessary.
6. Wrap dough in a plastic wrap.
7. Use the plastic to make the dough flat. Then press dough into a disk.
8. Refrigerate till it becomes firm. Often, it takes 120 minutes.
9. Heat oven to 180°C and place the rack in the lowest position.
10. Line a baking sheet with parchment.
11. On a lightly floured surface, roll 2 doughs to a length of 13 inches with a width of 18 inches in a rectangle shape.
12. Transfer to a pan and cut to an inch overhang. Tuck ends under.
13. Place in a refrigerator to chill.
14. Roll the rest of the dough to 1/4 inch thick.
15. Cut dough with cutters in the shape of flowers.
16. Transfer to prepared baking sheets.
17. Allow to cool.
18. Stir sugar, cornstarch, orange zest, and salt in a bowl.
19. Add the strawberries and orange juice and twirl gently to blend.
20. Transfer to a ground crust, bag tightly in a pan.
21. Whisk egg white and 2 teaspoons water together in a bowl.
22. Brush dough flowers with egg wash.
23. Arrange dough flower on top of strawberries.
24. Brush ends of dough with egg white.
25. Refrigerate for twenty minutes.
26. Bake on a large baking sheet made of aluminum until the crust turns golden brown.
27. Cool for half an hour before serving.

LEMON – BUTTER MILK TART

Serving: 8 people

Baking Time: 25 minutes

Plus Cooling time: 4 hours 10 minutes

Ingredients

2/3 cup of buttermilk

Half cup granulated sugar

2 large eggs

Half recipe basic pie dough

Quarter cup of lemon juice

2 tablespoons of light brown sugar

2 tablespoons unsalted butter, melted

1/8 teaspoon of kosher salt

2/3 buttermilk

Confectioners' sugar for dusting

Equipment

Pan

Parchment Paper

Tart Crust

Directions

1. Heat your oven to 270°C.
2. On the surface with flour, roll half basic pie dough to a circle of 11 inches.
3. Transfer dough to a tart pan of 9 inches. The pan should have a bottom that you can remove.
4. Squeeze dough into edges.
5. Tuck overhang into the pan and squeeze into flutes.
6. Chill for 15 minutes.
7. Line tart pan with parchment paper
8. Leave the overhang, and fill with dried beans.
9. Place on a baking sheet and transfer to oven.
10. Bake till ends turn brown.
11. Eliminate parchment and beans.
12. Bake till bottom turns light brown and dry. It takes 5 minutes to complete this process.
13. Whisk flour, buttermilk, granulated sugar, light brown sugar, lemon zest, butter, eggs, and salt.
14. Pour into warm tart crust.
15. Bake till filling is ready.
16. Remove and place on a rack to cool.
17. Remove tart ring and dust with the confectioners' sugar.

CRANBERRY – CHERRY COBBLER PIE

Serving: 8 people
Baking Time: 25 minutes
Plus Cooling Time: 85 minutes

Ingredients

1 tablespoon lime juice
1 teaspoon kosher salt, divide it
2 teaspoons baking
Half cup cold unsalted butter, cut up
3/4 cup buttermilk
340 g cranberries
340 g frozen sweet cherries
1 1/2 cup multi – purpose flour, spooned
Quarter cup of cornstarch
1 teaspoon lime zest grated

Equipment

9 inch Pie Plate
Baking Sheet

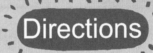
Directions

1. Heat oven to 280 degrees Celsius.
2. Whisk cornstarch, lime zest, half teaspoon of salt, 2/3 cup sugar together.
3. Add cranberries and cherries. Swirl to blend.
4. Transport to a pie plate that is 9 inches long.
5. Whisk flour, baking powder, remaining salt, and 2 tablespoons of sugar.
6. Cut butter into the recipe.
7. Continue till recipe looks like coarse meal.
8. Add buttermilk and slowly stir to mix.
9. Continue till mixture forms a wet, shaggy dough.
10. Add mounds of dough to the top of fruit.
11. Sprinkle with sugar.
12. Bake, using baking sheet.
13. Stop when it turns golden and bubbling.
14. Cool slightly.

BANANA TART TALIN

Serving: 6 people
Baking Time: 5 minutes
Plus Cooling time: 50 minutes

Ingredients

100g golden caster sugar
5 firm bananas
Pinch of sea salt
Orange (zest)
1 teaspoon cinnamon
1 tablespoon icing sugar
1 tablespoon dark rum
75g butter, cut into cube shapes.

Equipment

Pan
Cake Tin
Spoon
Large Plate

Directions

1. Heat the oven to 200C.
2. Melt both sugar and butter at the same time.
3. Use low heat without stirring the combination. Immediately the sugar melts, increase the heat till bubbles appear and turns deep caramel color.
4. If the butter separates itself from the caramel, remove the pan from the heat and add 1 tablespoon of water.
5. Stir till the butter becomes solid again.
6. Squirt the caramel into a cake tin of 23cm. The tin should have a solid base.
7. Spread the caramel quickly with a spoon around the cake tin.
8. Slice the bananas into two pieces. Arrange them in circles in the tin.
9. Then, sprinkle sea salt over them with half orange zest.
10. Slice the pastry into circles.
11. Lay the pastry on the banana top. Tuck the ends inside the tin.
12. Bake in the oven for half an hour till the pastry rises and cooks through.
13. Whisk the double cream and the icing sugar together till it forms soft perks.
14. Add rum, cinnamon, and the orange zest that is left. Whisk till everything blends well.
15. Allow the tart to cool in the cake tin. Then gently turn the tart onto a large plate. Make sure to wear oven gloves because the hot caramel splashes.
16. Use ice cream to serve your banana tart talin.

CHAPTER EIGHT

HEALTHY BAKED

PANNELET COOKIES WITH SWEET POTATO AND COCONUT

Serving: 8 people
Baking Time: 18 – 24 minutes
Plus Cooling Time: 40 minutes
Ingredients
Cinnamon
Baking powder
Grounded flaxseed
Vanilla extract
Shredded coconut
Eggs
Quick oats
Mashed potatoes
Coconut oil or butter

Equipment

Cookie sheets lined with parchment paper
Food processor
Oven

Directions

1. Take a medium bowl and whisk the egg whites, sugar, salt, shredded coconut, and mashed potatoes together.
2. Beat the almonds in a food processor.
3. Mix the almonds and the butter and make sure that everything is soft and sticky.
4. Let it cool for at least an hour allowing the coconut to absorb moisture from the potatoes.
5. Preheat the oven to 325°F and position the racks properly.
6. Place some parts of the soft dough in sugar and twirl into balls of about 1 1/4 inches
7. Position it on the lined or greased cookie sheets.
8. Bake between 18 to 24 minutes, until the cookies are slightly crusty on the surface.
9. To ensure even baking, roll the pans from top to bottom and from front to back.
10. Cool the cookies completely before storing.
11. You can keep the cookies in an airtight container for up to 4 or 5 days.

FRUITY BERRY TARTS WITH VANILLA CASHEW CREAM

Serving: 4 People
Baking Time: 25 minutes
Plus Cooling Time: 50 minutes

Ingredients

Half cup raw almonds, soaked for at least four hours
Half cup raw cashews, soaked for at least four hours
Eight medjool dates
Quarter teaspoon pint of salt
Two tablespoon vanilla extract
Three tablespoon maple butter
Two tablespoon coconut milk
One tablespoon of melted coconut oil.
Fruits
Strawberries
Blueberries
Blackberries
Raspberries
Kiwis

Equipment

Blender
art Pan

Directions

1. Soak and dry the nuts
2. Pour all the fruit ingredients into a blender and blend properly.
3. Pour out into a tart pan and spread the mixture out to form a crust.
4. Place in the freezer to cool and start making the vanilla cashew cream.
5. Add the cashew cream ingredients to the blender and blend properly.
6. While it is still blending, pour the coconut oil into the mixture slowly.
7. Bring out the crust from the freezer and add it to the cashew cream.
8. Put the mixture inside the fridge for at least an hour.
9. Arrange the berries and kiwi slices around the tart.
10. Add your honey to help hold the berries and give your creation a sparkling glow.

GLUTEN FREE LEMON BARS

Serving: 24 Bars
Baking Time: 25 minutes
Plus Cooling Time: 45 minutes

Ingredients

Butter
Granulated sugar
Gluten Free Flour
Eggs
Baking powder
Finely shredded lemon zest
or lemon juice

Equipment:

Bowls
Pan

Directions

1. Preheat the oven to 325°F and cover the baking pan with parchment paper.
2. Use a large bowl to blend the melted butter, vanilla extract, salt and sugar.
3. Add the gluten-free flour and stir properly to mix together.
4. Roll the dough that forms in the lined pan.
5. Bake for 25 minutes or until the dough is lightly browned.
6. Remove from the oven and set aside.

Lemon Filling

1. Whisk eggs, sugar, lemon juice and vanilla extract in a large bowl.
2. Add the gluten-free flour and whisk properly to form fully.
3. Sprinkle the whole lemon filling on the warm crust.
4. Bake for about 26 minutes.
5. Remove the bar from the oven leave to cool for an hour.
6. Place in the refrigerator before you serve.

MOCHI - COVERED STRAWBER RIES

Serving: 8 People
Baking Time: 22 minutes
Plus Cooling Time: 50 minutes

Ingredients

Mochiko (a sweet rice flour)
Sugar
Potato starch
Strawberries
Koshian (a sweet red or
white bean paste)

Equipment

Cooking pot
Parchment paper
Microwave

Directions

1. Mix mochiko, sugar, and water in a small bowl.
2. Wrap it with foil parchment.
3. Fill a large pot and close it with a tight-fitting lid.
4. Steam until mixture is transparent and gummy, for about 22 minutes.
5. Remove pot lid and stir mixture until it is thick and a dough forms.
6. Add strawberries all over with bean paste.
7. Sprinkle the surface with potato starch.
8. Swab with more starch and cut into 8 pieces.
9. Encase the strawberry with a piece of mochi by rolling it with your palm to remove excess starch.
10. Repeat the process with mochi and strawberries.
11. Always serve at room temperature, and eat within 48 hours.

GRANOLA BARK

Serving: 16 People
Baking Time: 10 - 15 minutes
Plus Cooling Time: 30 minutes

Ingredients

½ cup of maple syrup
½ cup of coconut sugar
¼ cup of water
2 teaspoons of vanilla extract
1/2 teaspoon of salt
3 cups of rolled oats
Chopped uncooked almonds
¾ cup of shredded coconut
1/2 cup of almond flour or whole flour
6 teaspoon of grounded cinnamon
80ml vegetable oil
1 egg white
35g sesame seeds

Equipment

Bowls
Baking Pan
Parchment Paper
Baking Sheet
Airtight Container

Directions

1. Mix the maple syrup, sugar, water, vanilla, and salt in a small bowl
2. Add boiling water, and stir to dissolve the sugar and salt and allow it to cool to lukewarm temperatures.
3. Preheat the oven to 325°F and line a baking pan with parchment paper.
4. Bring a large bowl, and mix the oats, almonds, shredded coconut, whole flour, flax meal, sesame seeds, and cinnamon together.
5. Add the egg white and maple syrup mixture.
6. Pour the wet mixture on the oats mixture and blend properly.
7. Spread out the mixture on the baking sheets.
8. Bake for about 40 minutes or till it appears golden brown
9. Rotate the sheet every 10-15 minutes to avoid burns.
10. Remove the pan from the oven and allow it to cool.
11. Store in a refrigerator or airtight container

CONCLUSION

We all want our kids to develop interest in baking. The amazing news is that they also want to. Acting on it is often the hard part. We are always looking for recipes that kids will enjoy. This book contains a lot of them.

And my cute ones, all your favorite recipes are here! Without having to disturb mommy all the time, you can begin baking right away. I'm sure you already found one that you love.

Why not start baking right away.

Printed in Great Britain
by Amazon

31702234R00086